Prayers
of
Hope for
Caregivers

SARAH FORGRAVE

HARVEST HOUSE PUBLISHERS
EUGENE, OREGON

Cover design by Aesthetic Soup

Cover image © GhostArt/Shutterstock

Backcover author photo by Christian Barreno

Published in association with Books & Such Literary Management, 52 Mission Circle, Suite 122, PMB 170, Santa Rosa, CA 95409-5370, www.booksandsuch.com.

Prayers of Hope for Caregivers
Copyright © 2019 by Sarah Forgrave
Published by Harvest House Publishers
Eugene, Oregon 97408
www.harvesthousepublishers.com

ISBN 978-0-7369-7577-3 (hardcover)
ISBN 978-0-7369-7578-0 (eBook)

Library of Congress Cataloging-in-Publication Data

Names: Forgrave, Sarah, author.
Title: Prayers of hope for caregivers / Sarah Forgrave.
Description: Eugene, Oregon : Harvest House Publishers, [2018]
Identifiers: LCCN 2018025865 (print) | LCCN 2018039143 (ebook) | ISBN 9780736975780 (ebook) | ISBN 9780736975773 (hardcover) | ISBN 9780736975780 (ebk.)
Subjects: LCSH: Caregivers--Prayers and devotions.
Classification: LCC BV4910.9 (ebook) | LCC BV4910.9 .F67 2018 (print) | DDC 242/.4--dc23
LC record available at https://lccn.loc.gov/2018025865

Printed in China
19 20 21 22 23 24 25 26 27 / RDS-GL / 10 9 8 7 6 5 4 3 2 1

*For the doctors and medical staff who have
cared for my family over the years—*

You are true heroes and servants.

———ٯٯ٧———

And for my sister—

This book wouldn't exist without you.

Contents

An Invitation to Rest

If there's one phrase that comes to mind when I think of caregivers, it's *selfless servants*. From my vantage point, no calling in life requires more strength, sacrifice, stamina, and patience than caring for someone with physical needs.

After writing my book *Prayers for Hope and Healing*, I received feedback from many readers who didn't face a medical challenge themselves but who struggled through the turmoil of someone else's illness. A grandma feeling helpless as she supported her twentysomething daughter through the loss of a baby. A wife watching her husband go into open-heart surgery. An empty-nest daughter caring for her mother and trying to hide the depth of burden she carried.

These heartaches and so many others fill the pages of our lives. And yet, as caregivers and loved ones close to the crisis, we're often forgotten in the shadow of the sick.

While I haven't carried the burden of providing long-term support for an aging parent or disabled family member—two requirements that often come to mind when I hear the term *caregiver*—my life has been filled with the medical crises of family members. I've served as a short-term caregiver and watched others provide ongoing support to those close to me.

It started when I was a young child. My teenaged sister battled cancer for four years until her illness culminated in a bone marrow transplant. Going into the transplant, she was given a 10% chance of survival, and she beat the predictions.

While I didn't fully grasp her condition at my young age, I knew her sickness could send her to heaven at any moment. The stress it put on my parents was palpable, even though they did everything possible to lessen its impact on my brother and me.

As I transitioned to adulthood, life settled into a comfortable pattern. But after having two children and facing medical challenges of my own, I found myself back in the hospital with my sister. Her chemotherapy from years ago had damaged her heart, and the only way to survive was a transplant. She was admitted to a hospital near my home and set up camp indefinitely until a new heart became available. Because her husband and daughter lived three hours away, I visited her every day of her seven weeks of hospitalization.

After receiving her new heart, she lived with me for

the month following before she was released to go home. That month was downright daunting at times. Anxiety swelled as I navigated germ control with two young children. Exhaustion set in as I prepared meals that suited varying dietary needs. Relationships shifted with additional houseguests coming and going. But through it all, God filled me with the strength I needed.

Not long after that challenging season, my son faced a medical crisis. A severe infection rapidly formed in his jaw, sending him to the emergency room on his first day of second grade. The situation was serious. It was the first time I've been ushered straight back without seeing the waiting room. If his infection spread to his neck, it would block his air passage.

While I stood in the small holding room of the ER, calming my panic-prone son and waiting for doctors to analyze his CT scan, I did the only thing I could. I prayed. My prayers weren't eloquent or flowery, but in them I pleaded with God to save my son, to give the doctors wisdom, and to give me supernatural peace in the meantime.

As my son was wheeled into emergency surgery in the middle of the night and spent the next two days in the ICU, I found myself returning to that place of prayer over and over again because nothing else in this world felt stable. My pleas were uttered in sputters and spurts, but I knew God heard and understood.

Whether your caregiving role is short term or a long, arduous journey, you've likely carried a similar burden. Pastors and friends have perhaps prayed for the situation, focusing their attention on the sick or injured while you feel the aftershocks of their pain with no safe outlet to express them.

That very struggle is what prompted me to write this book.

Using my own experiences and those close to me who have filled a long-term caregiving role, I've created a collection of devotions and prayers to meet you where you are. You're welcome to read the book from front to back, or it can be used as a menu of sorts. When a particular emotion or struggle hits, let the table of contents lead you to the page you need. (For the sake of simplicity, I've alternated references to the care recipient as *he* and *she* throughout the book. Feel free to substitute as needed to fit your situation.)

As you read, I pray you'll sense God's love and peace. Even when you're exhausted from bearing this burden, He offers a place of rest.

I pray you'll lean into Him during this trying time.

Sarah

1

When There's No End in Sight

For those helping someone in a long-term
health struggle.

Give me neither poverty nor riches,
but give me only my daily bread.

PROVERBS 30:8

———⁓⁓⁓———

Your calendar is filled with days and months, each one like the last. This process of caring for someone has no foreseeable end, even though you've reached the end of your limits multiple times.

Perhaps you have a child with a disability requiring frequent doctor visits. Maybe you're caring for a wounded warrior with limited mobility. Or maybe you're the guardian of aging parents who have a decade of life ahead of them, but whose independence dwindles a little more each day.

No matter your circumstances, I pray you'll remember that next week, next month, and next year are in God's hands. You can rest in this moment and feed on the daily bread He provides. When you see an endless stretch of challenges, your heavenly Father draws you close. He promises to restore you in His perfect timing.

Will you let Him do that now?

—\~—

Dear Lord,

I'm struggling to stay positive when this role seems never ending. Not only am I physically exhausted, but my emotions and spirit are worn out too. At times I want to know when all of this will end, but I'm also scared of that day because it means losing someone I love.

As my energy fades, would You renew me with Your strength? I recognize I can't get through this alone, so keep me grounded in You. Thank You for the reminder that I don't need to dwell on the poverty or riches of this situation, but You've provided what I need for today.

When my mind races ahead to the length of this process—when discouragement and exhaustion threaten to pull me under—open my eyes to see the bread You've given me in this moment. I want to be grateful for Your provision rather than grumbling about my struggles.

Keep me connected to You so I can remain aware of what my care recipient needs. When I feel as if I have nothing left to give, show me what to do next, whether I need to press through the pain, ask for help, or give myself permission to rest.

I want to be a light for You, Lord, so fill me with purpose and joy as I interact with other caregivers and medical personnel. Help me use this season to reflect Your love, rather than shrinking into the cave of my hardship. Give me fresh perspective and courage of heart.

The days ahead may seem endless, but Father, You are eternal. I'm grateful You're not limited by space and time, and I praise You for providing what I need right now.

In Jesus's name, amen.

2

When You Can't Sleep

For those who need rest but find
themselves lying awake.

*Come to me, all you who are weary and burdened,
and I will give you rest.*

MATTHEW 11:28

———

Y ou toss and turn, but sleep is nowhere to be found.
How are you supposed to care for someone when
you can't refill your tank?

Rest may elude you for many reasons. You might be
woken in the night to administer medicine or calm the
cries of someone in pain. You may be sleeping on a stiff
hospital couch, with nurse visits interrupting your rest
every two hours. Perhaps you're called upon to work the
night shift, and your body can't adjust.

Whatever the cause, let the words of Jesus draw you

to Him. He doesn't guarantee you won't face weariness in this life, but He does promise to lessen its weight. When sleep is elusive, He invites you to renew your soul in His presence—to settle in the deep, restorative cushion of His care.

Will you accept the invitation?

———※———

Dear Lord,

I'm so tired of feeling weary. During a season when I need to be strong for someone else, it seems as if circumstances keep working against me. Countless tasks, noises, and interruptions collide with a million thoughts racing through my head. The lack of sleep isn't just taxing me physically, but it's fraying my emotions too. My patience has worn thin, and frustration sits constantly at the edge of my spirit, ready to boil over.

Lord, I ask forgiveness for the times I've allowed my weariness to hurt those close to me. I recognize we're all impacted by this situation, and I don't want to lose sight of the struggle of others. Enable me to make things right where needed, and restore any cracks in my relationships.

If I need to change something around me to facilitate

better sleep, help me see that. When I'm tempted to rely on my own strength, slow me down to rest in You. This season may not be easy, but You promise to provide what I need.

Thank You for accepting me as I am and inviting me to lay my burdens at Your feet. It's a gift I've often neglected, but I want this to be a new start. I come to You as I am and ask for Your help. I trust that even in this longing for sleep, You'll quiet my heart. Turn my thoughts to Your goodness, and settle me in a place of gratitude and peace.

Whether sleep comes or not, I pray You would loosen the tension in my mind and spirit. I want a soul that's revived for the work ahead of me, and I rely on You alone to renew me.

In Jesus's name, amen.

3

When You Don't Understand God's Plan

For those who struggle to see why God would allow anyone to suffer.

This is what the Lord says: "You will be in Babylon for seventy years. But then I will come and do for you all the good things I have promised, and I will bring you home again. For I know the plans I have for you," says the Lord. "They are plans for good and not for disaster, to give you a future and a hope. In those days when you pray, I will listen. If you look for me wholeheartedly, you will find me. I will be found by you," says the Lord. "I will end your captivity and restore your fortunes. I will gather you out of the nations where I sent you and will bring you home again to your own land."

JEREMIAH 29:10-14 NLT

―――∽∽―――

Suffering surrounds you until your spirit shifts. No longer do you face this situation with acceptance. Uncertainty has taken hold and won't let go. You may feel like a captive, watching your care recipient struggle through physical hardship. Her burden becomes yours, and questions build in your spirit until they threaten to bury you.

How can this be part of a loving God's plan? Is He watching? Does He care?

As you face these doubts, I pray you'll draw comfort from Scripture. A verse often quoted in churches—"I know the plans I have for you"—is accompanied by seventy years of captivity.

When you're in the midst of life's chains, you may struggle to see any purpose. But God promises He's working for your good. He's made plans to "end your captivity and restore your fortunes." During this difficult time, He invites you to come to Him. To pray and search for Him with your whole heart. To trust that He listens and cares.

Will you turn to Him now?

—∿—

Dear Lord,

I feel so trapped in this situation as I watch suffering

day after day. Not only has it drained my energy and time, but it's eroded my trust in You. How could this be part of Your plan? I read Bible verses that say You work all things for good, but I question whether it's possible.

Even as I sift through my doubts, I long to believe Your promises are true. I want to know You'll bring healing in this situation, that You'll give me a future and a hope. I recognize that my care recipient probably struggles with similar questions, so I ask for extra faith so I can be an encouragement to her. Give us opportunities to talk through our doubts and fears together, and open a channel of communication that ultimately flows to You in prayer.

Thank You for Your promise to listen when I come to You. May I never forget that Your presence is with me at all times. Even though I don't understand Your bigger plan, I choose to trust You anyway. Take away my mask when I'm tempted to cover my doubts. I know You already see what's in my heart, and I thank You for that. Help me to come to You as I am, to seek truth in Scripture rather than feeding my fears alone.

I may not understand how You could end this captivity or restore my fortunes, but I place it all in Your hands. I ask You to take this situation and use it for Your glory.

In Jesus's name, amen.

4

When You Feel Abandoned by Your Friends

For those who've dropped off their friends' priority lists.

I look for someone to come and help me, but no one gives me a passing thought! No one will help me; no one cares a bit what happens to me. Then I pray to you, O LORD. I say, "You are my place of refuge. You are all I really want in life."

PSALM 142:4-5 NLT

[God] has never let you down, never looked the other way when you were being kicked around. He has never wandered off to do his own thing; he has been right there, listening.

PSALM 22:24 MSG

Y ou glance at your phone and wonder if anyone remembers you. Your friends aren't all that far away, but your paths don't cross as often as they used to.

While a few people have stepped in to help in meaningful ways, others seem to have disappeared completely. Your world has turned upside down, and they've fallen off the face of the earth. Maybe they've focused their attention on your care recipient, or perhaps they've failed to reach out at all. Maybe they've checked in once or twice, but with a hurried message that says they don't have time to listen.

Whatever the case, you're left feeling the brunt of their silence.

My friend, while those close to you may disappear, remember you're not forgotten by your heavenly Father. He's never been too busy with His agenda to forget about you. He's never looked away from your problems or tried to minimize the struggle. He's here with you now, and He's listening.

As you meet Him in your hurt, He offers a place of refuge. He longs to soothe you with His presence.

Will you lean into Him now?

Dear Lord,

Caregiving has cut me off from my friends, and I'll admit it hurts. It feels as if I've entered an alternate universe, and they've moved on with their lives as though I don't exist. My time is consumed with new responsibilities, and though I know it's hard for others to understand the stress I'm under, it would be nice to hear from them and know they care.

Father, as I struggle with the hurt, would You grant me grace to see my friends from Your perspective? I recognize they may not be ignoring me on purpose. They're likely trying to keep up with their own schedules, or they're not sure what to say or how to help. Whatever the cause, I don't want their silence to erode my knowledge of who I am in You.

Your Word says You are never too busy for me, that You'll never run off to do Your own thing. What a comfort that is, especially during this time. I ask You to make Your presence real to me in this moment. Allow me to use this season to draw close to You. I lean on Your promises and trust You to fill the empty places inside.

I also ask for wisdom and courage to reach out to others if needed. If You want me to seek restoration with someone who has hurt me, grant me the right words.

If You have new friendships in store, open my eyes to see them, and give me the faith to follow through.

No matter what happens in my relationships on earth, I want You to be my highest priority. Help me seek You first and rest in Your presence alone.

In Jesus's name, amen.

5

When You Feel Angry

For those who are angry about their situation
and ultimately at God.

*When Mary reached the place where Jesus was and saw
him, she fell at his feet and said, "Lord, if you had been
here, my brother would not have died." When Jesus saw
her weeping, and the Jews who had come along with her
also weeping, he was deeply moved in spirit and troubled.
"Where have you laid him?" he asked. "Come and see,
Lord," they replied. Jesus wept.*

JOHN 11:32-35

—⁂—

J esus wept." The shortest verse in the Bible, but it
speaks volumes.

This story shows the heart of God in the midst of
pain. A sister, heartbroken at the loss of her brother,
expresses her frustration and hurt. Her words are spoken

in anguish, but there's an undercurrent of anger. *If you had been here…*

And yet, Jesus doesn't condemn her for her honesty. He weeps alongside her.

My friend, you may have similar emotions coursing through your veins. You may be angry at God for not being there when you've needed Him. You might hurl insults as you watch someone in your care suffer.

Whether you've expressed your feelings to God or you've stuffed them inside, trust that He's deeply moved by your struggle. He doesn't condemn you for questioning, but He does want to meet you here and bring you to a place of faith.

Will you allow Him to do that?

—⚬—

Dear Lord,

I'll admit I'm struggling with anger toward You. My life has been filled with so many challenges, and I can't see any glimpses of Your presence. I relate to Mary in the Bible all too well. There are times I want to blame You for not working the way I want. "If only…" is at the tip of my tongue as I watch my care recipient suffer. It doesn't seem fair to put us through this.

I'm grateful that even as I grapple with these emotions, Your Word reminds me I'm not alone. You gave Mary permission to express her anguish, and You do the same for me. Help me accept Your gift in a way that honors You. I want to be honest in my prayer life, but if anger pushes me to sin against You or others, please fill me with humility to recognize my error.

Enable me to go deeper so I can pinpoint the true source of my anger. If fear is involved, I lay my worries at Your feet. If grief is the cause, draw me to You for comfort. Where pride is driving my actions, remind me that You alone are in control of this situation, and You're working in my pain.

Thank You for meeting me in this place, especially as I face emotions that aren't always pretty. You accept me as I am, and You mourn and weep with me. Remind me of Your love when my anger rises, and fill me with a deep, abiding trust.

In Jesus's name, amen.

6

When You Feel Caught in an Endless Cycle

For those who are working tirelessly but have nothing to show for it.

After you have suffered a little while, the God of all grace, who has called you to his eternal glory in Christ, will himself restore, confirm, strengthen, and establish you.

1 Peter 5:10 esv

———— ⁓⁓ ————

Another day of caregiving slogs by like the day before. Endless needs, appointments, and challenges lie ahead, blurring with such familiarity that they've become routine—a routine you wish were different. This role has turned out to be more selfless than you imagined. More time consuming and tiring. In other areas of life, you see tangible evidence of your labor. But in this season, your work never ends, and the rewards are few and far between.

Dear friend, as you struggle through this cycle, I pray you're encouraged by reminders of God's grace. Suffering may last for a time, but He has an eternal glory in mind for you. When you feel broken, lost, and weak, your heavenly Father is making plans to restore and strengthen you—to set you on a firm foundation.

He alone can establish you and give you hope. He holds out His hand, offering all you need.

Will you take hold of Him and rest in His presence?

―᚜᚜᚜―

Dear Lord,

This season has tested my strength and patience. Facing the same tasks day after day has left me worn out. Sometimes I feel as if I'm stuck on a treadmill with the belt spinning beneath my feet. I'm going nowhere, and yet my energy wanes and my muscles tire from the effort to stay upright.

As I face the challenges ahead, I'm so grateful You haven't left me alone. When my life feels stuck on "repeat," You're working to restore my strength and hope. Would You remind me of this when I doubt?

Lord, I ask for renewed energy to provide what my care recipient needs. I know he's likely discouraged from being trapped in this cycle too, so I pray You would sustain both of us during this time. Keep us unified as we face each day.

I also pray for open eyes to see the needs of those around me. As I visit the same doctors' offices or interact with the same nursing home staff, let me shine for You. If there's an opportunity to share the hope of eternal life, grant me the right words. I want others to see an active faith in the midst of my suffering, and it will only happen through Your Holy Spirit.

Fill me with awareness of Your presence here and now. My circumstances may not change, but I know You can breathe new life into my soul. I ask for that outpouring today.

Thank You for Your promise of restoration and strength. I lean into You and anticipate the ways You will move in my life.

In Jesus's name, amen.

7

When You Feel Far from God

For those who feel that God doesn't care
about their situation.

My God, my God, why have you abandoned me?
Why are you so far away when I groan for help?

PSALM 22:1 NLT

The LORD is near to all who call on him,
to all who call on him in truth.

PSALM 145:18

Emptiness gapes in your soul as you face each day.
You go about your tasks, but deep inside you ache
for signs of God's presence but see none. As your care
recipient suffers, you might question if God is good or
whether He's here at all. If He has the power to heal,
why doesn't He remove this burden? Why doesn't He
offer relief?

My friend, these questions may pile up inside, but rest assured your heavenly Father welcomes you as you are. In this psalm, David poured out his struggle to his Savior. He held nothing back as he groaned for help, trapped in a state of absolute loneliness. Yet he was able to say with confidence, "The LORD is near."

Your situation may not change, but you can always call out to God. He longs to make His presence real to you, to offer peace for your soul.

Will you let Him?

——— ✺ ———

Dear Lord,

This season has caused me to question so much, leaving me to wonder if You're still here. My days are filled with exhausting work, and I feel the gap in my soul widening. I've struggled to see You in the midst of it all—to believe You see me and care.

Father, this numbness of spirit isn't a fun way to live, and I can't stay here forever. Would You give me a glimpse of Your presence? As I sift through my questions, please open my eyes to see You working. I may not know how this will end, but I want to believe You haven't left me to fend for myself.

Thank You for reminding me I'm not alone in this

struggle. Your anointed one, King David, expressed his hurt and questioned Your plan. I'm grateful for his model of honesty and ultimate faith in You.

As I come to You now, I ask for a pure heart. I don't want to come to You selfishly, demanding that You wave a magic wand and make things better. While I would love to see a miraculous healing for my care recipient—and I ask You to do that if it's in Your will—what I want above all is to know You more deeply.

Do a mighty work in me, and help me seek after You when questions loom. As I fill my mind with Your Word, enable me to stand firm in the truth You reveal. I never want to lose sight of Your love, so I bring my hurts and trust You to draw near.

In Jesus's name, amen.

8

When You Feel Inadequate

For those who can't provide what's needed.

He said to me, "My grace is sufficient for you, for my power is made perfect in weakness." Therefore I will boast all the more gladly about my weaknesses, so that Christ's power may rest on me.

2 CORINTHIANS 12:9

I can do everything through Christ, who gives me strength.

PHILIPPIANS 4:13 NLT

————

No matter where you turn, something begs for your attention. Many different roles fill the hours of your day—chauffeur, nurse, housekeeper, chef, arbitrator, money manager, and more. Some of these may come to you with ease, while others stretch you out of your comfort zone. Maybe your abilities are up to the task, but your calendar isn't. Whatever the case, you're faced with the reality that you can't do it all.

When you tackle a task that feels impossible, remember you have a heavenly Father with no limits. He offers unending grace to see you through. In fact, He promises to work through your weakness in ways that exceed human bounds.

Do you believe His power can rest on you in this moment? His God-sized strength is yours for the taking. You may feel inadequate, but He provides everything you need.

Will you seek His help now?

———ᨆ———

Dear Lord,

It's so humbling to acknowledge I have limits. Sometimes I feel pulled in a dozen directions, and it's just a matter of time before I break. Other days, I have a good handle on my tasks, but then something new arises and sends me into a tailspin. Not only do I lack physical strength, but I struggle to provide what's needed emotionally and spiritually too.

Lord, as I face this inadequacy, I'm grateful You can shine through my weakness. I ask You to work in me now. Calm my mind and heart to prioritize what's needed, and enable me to call on others for help. I pray for a team of people to surround me who can fill in the gaps. If there's a new skill I can learn, show me what to do and reveal the next steps I need to take.

When I receive unrealistic demands from my care recipient, I pray for an extra measure of grace. I recognize her life has been upended by this struggle, and I'm an easy outlet for her frustration. Allow us to communicate openly so we can right any wrongs. Soften my heart to forgive with the same forgiveness You've shown me.

Above all, thank You for offering Your power to me during this time. What an amazing privilege—to have heavenly strength flowing through me. When I'm tempted to rely on my own abilities, I lift my eyes to You. Your ways are higher than mine, and I trust You to provide what I need.

In Jesus's name, amen.

9

When You Feel Invisible

For those who feel lost in the shadow of the sick.

In my distress I called to the LORD;
I cried to my God for help.
From his temple he heard my voice;
my cry came before him, into his ears.

PSALM 18:6

———

It's happened yet again. A well-meaning friend or acquaintance has asked about your care recipient, while you stand by and wonder, "Don't I matter too?" As you pour yourself out for someone else, you may feel forgotten. Invisible.

Maybe your care recipient is so covered in prayer that he's nestled in a place of peace. A giant bubble of grace surrounds him, sustaining him through this trial, but you're left on the outside. You find yourself fighting exhaustion and weakness with no armor to stand firm—no prayer circle girding you with strength.

My friend, when it seems as though everyone looks past you, remember that you're seen and loved by God. He offers comfort not only to your care recipient; He offers comfort to *you*. This season may leave you feeling invisible, but you can always call on your Savior. He promises to listen, care, and provide.

Will you turn to Him now?

—⁓—

Dear Lord,

I feel selfish praying this prayer, but the truth is, I wonder if anyone sees me. I know my care recipient's needs are great, and it makes sense that people are concerned about him. But it would be nice to know they're thinking of me too. When they ask how he's doing or how they can pray for him, I want to add my own needs. Yet I don't want to sound self-absorbed, as if my struggle is more important than his.

Father, what a relief to know that even though people may look past me, You notice everything. You see my challenges and lack of strength. You know the emotional burden I carry, and You don't judge me for needing help.

Remind me of this when I feel alone. I'm so grateful for Your listening ear, for the invitation to call to You in my time of distress. I don't want to stay buried in this hardship without turning to You, so I ask for a heart that seeks You first.

I also know how valuable earthly friendships can be. As I walk this journey, help me recognize the people nearby who can offer support and encouragement. I don't want to be afraid or feel guilty to ask for prayer, so grant me the faith to reach out. Surround me with a prayer circle, even if it's one or two close friends, and show me how I can come alongside them in return.

No matter what happens, I choose to turn to You. Whether anyone sees my struggle or not, I believe You know my needs. I commit to coming to You first for my comfort and strength.

In Jesus's name, amen.

10

When You Feel Misunderstood

For those who feel as if no one understands
their burden.

The LORD appeared to us in the past, saying:
"I have loved you with an everlasting love;
I have drawn you with unfailing kindness."

JEREMIAH 31:3

We know and rely on the love God has for us. God is love.
Whoever lives in love lives in God, and God in them.

1 JOHN 4:16

You look around and wonder if anyone understands your struggle. Every moment of exhaustion, heartache, and pain seems to push you further onto a ledge of isolation.

Perhaps your friends minimize the burden you face

when you try to open up to them. Maybe you hear others' opinions on how to proceed with your care recipient, but they don't know all the implications. Or maybe the misunderstanding comes directly from the person under your care, when she fails to recognize the load weighing you down.

Wherever you find yourself, I pray you're comforted by the promises in God's Word. When people disappoint you on earth, you have a heavenly Father who is faithful. He draws you to Himself with unfailing kindness. He sees and knows your hardship.

His love has no boundaries or limits—no judgment or scorn. It's a love you can *rest in* and *rely on*.

Will you meet Him here now?

—~—

Dear Lord,

I find myself alone in so many ways. The burden I carry is heavy, but it weighs deeper when others don't seem to understand my struggle. They might mean well when they minimize my challenges or try to give their opinion, but it still bothers me. I'm doing the best I can in these circumstances, and I would love for someone to come alongside me and seek to understand.

Lord, even when others miss the mark, I'm grateful You see me fully. I'll admit I get wrapped up in my struggle and forget You're here. When I place my worth in other people's responses, draw me back to You. I recognize I can't stay hidden in my shell, and I want to interact with others in a way that brings You glory. When frustration threatens to leak out in hurtful ways, rein me in. Fill me with humility to recognize if I need to reach across the bridge and reconcile.

If the source of misunderstanding is outsiders who are too busy to listen, I pray for grace to see them through Your eyes. I don't want to ask for more than they can give, so keep me in balance when I lose perspective. If someone inserts an opinion of what I should do—whether a decision I'm weighing or a treatment plan for my care recipient—fill me with wisdom and confidence to move forward where You lead.

When I feel misunderstood by my care recipient, enable me to handle the situation with You as my guide. This relationship consumes so much time and energy. I don't want to do anything that creates irreparable damage. If I need to confront the situation, give me the right words and keep me in step with You regardless of my care recipient's response.

Whether I feel understood by others or not, I want to rest in Your love. Thank You for drawing me near and filling me with Your presence. I lean into You now.

In Jesus's name, amen.

11

When You Get Bad News

For those facing a poor prognosis for someone
under their care.

Cast all your anxiety on him because he cares for you.
1 PETER 5:7

I know the LORD is always with me.
I will not be shaken, for he is right beside me.
PSALM 16:8 NLT

———∿∿∿———

O ne phone call is all it takes to send you down a new
path of worries, needs, and challenges. Maybe
you've been caregiving for a while, and this prognosis
adds another layer of responsibilities. Perhaps the news
has launched you into a caregiver role for the first time.

Whether the road ahead is long or short, you're likely
facing a multitude of questions. *What does this mean for*

my care recipient? Will he make it through? Where do I fit in all of this, and am I up to the task?

Dear friend, as these worries swirl through your mind, remember you have a Savior who hears each one. Anxious thoughts may choke your trust, but God invites you to bring them to Him. He wants you to cast every concern onto His shoulders so He can carry the burden for you.

When you feel alone, He covers you with His love. When your world is shaken, He offers a stable hand to see you through. He remains with you through every turn of life.

Will you look to Him now?

—◈—

Dear Lord,

I know life isn't guaranteed to be happy and perfect, but it doesn't make it easier to hear this prognosis. So many thoughts are rushing through my mind. I'm worried about my care recipient and how he will get through this. The days ahead won't be easy for him as he seeks healing. I'm also worried about my role in providing care. At times it seems like too much to bear, and I don't feel up to the challenge.

As I navigate these fears, would You soothe me with Your peace? It's not easy to see how You could work in this situation, but I know You're moving. When anxiety rises, remind me that You carry my burden. I believe You can handle whatever comes next, so help me turn my concerns over to You each day.

I also ask for physical strength as I enter this new phase. Whatever lies ahead, You offer Your power to keep me going. If my care recipient needs more than I'm able to provide, guide me to the right people who can partner with me.

Fill me with the energy I need, but also with the emotional strength to support my care recipient. He's likely battling his own fears about the future, so I pray for wisdom to answer his questions and lead him to You. Draw both of us to You in prayer as we face the days ahead.

More than anything, Father, I want to stay grounded in Your presence. You offer a steadying hand, and I reach out to You now for my comfort and help.

In Jesus's name, amen.

12

When You Have to Cause Pain

For those who need to do what's best for their care recipient even if it's painful.

You will keep in perfect peace those whose minds are steadfast, because they trust in you. Trust in the LORD forever, for the LORD, the LORD himself, is the Rock eternal.

ISAIAH 26:3-4

The last thing you want to do is cause pain, but you have no choice. Perhaps you need to administer shots or drive your care recipient to a medical procedure that will leave her hurting. Maybe you have to cause pain in the form of limited independence—moving a parent into a nursing home or taking away her car keys.

If she's aware of your actions, she may lash out at you openly or accuse you passively with her silence. Perhaps outsiders will question your decision, driving the nail deeper in your spirit. It's not as if you want to create hardship, but you know it's necessary for your care recipient's well-being.

While you struggle through this situation, I pray you'll find comfort in God's steadfast love. He's the Solid Rock for a heart in turmoil. He gives perfect peace to the mind in doubt. He can be trusted in all places and times, even this one where you find yourself.

Will you turn your struggle over to Him?

———ɷ———

Dear Lord,

I'm torn up inside over this action I need to take. On the one hand, I know it's necessary and for the best. On the other hand, it's incredibly hard to cause someone pain. At times I envision my care recipient healthy and whole, and I question if I'm making the right choice. Other times I'm confident, but I hear doubts from others. My mind gets pulled in so many directions that it's hard to stay calm.

As I follow through, I know I can't do it without Your strength. When I feel the earth shifting beneath me, remind me that You're the Rock eternal. When doubts seep into my mind, flood me with reassurance.

If I'm moving forward too hastily, please slow me down to listen to Your guidance. I don't want to cause unnecessary pain, so I ask for a check in my spirit if I'm doing the wrong thing. If I'm on the right path but struggling to do what's best, fill me with courage. When others question the wisdom of my choice, keep me steadfast in the knowledge that this is where You've led me.

I pray for an extra measure of grace to cover my care recipient during this time. I know it won't be easy for her, and I want to help however I can. Fill me with the right words to communicate what's happening, so I can share in a way that expresses the need but also honors her dignity.

Whatever response I receive, I ask You to fill me with peace. I'm so grateful for Your guiding hand, and I trust You to work all things for good.

In Jesus's name, amen.

13

When You Have to Make a Hard Choice

For those making a weighty decision for someone under their care.

The Spirit of the LORD will rest on him—
the Spirit of wisdom and understanding,
the Spirit of counsel and might, the Spirit of
knowledge and the fear of the LORD.

ISAIAH 11:2 NLT

———⟨⟨⟨———

Multiple routes fan out before you, and you're fully aware that your choice will have ripple effects. Whether you're picking the right treatment plan for your care recipient or making decisions that will impact his home life, it's daunting to know which way to go. What if you make the wrong choice? What if it causes more harm than good? Will you be blamed for any fallout?

My friend, as you work through this decision, remember you have a heavenly Guide working in and through you. He'll help you sift through the pros and cons, and He'll open your eyes to see the impact.

When you feel uncertain, invite His wisdom to point the way. He may not show you the big picture, but He can give you confidence for the next step. As you fill your mind with truth, He promises to provide knowledge, counsel, and might. This isn't the promise of a human expert. It's spoken by the Almighty Creator. A God with unmatched understanding and strength.

Will you seek your answers in Him?

—⁓—

Dear Lord,

I'm at a crossroads, struggling to know which way to go. So many implications are at stake, and I admit it's overwhelming. Sometimes I want to get the decision over with and move on. Other times I feel paralyzed, worried I'll send my care recipient in the wrong direction. Questions abound, but I know I can't stay in limbo forever.

Father, as I work through this choice, would You be my guide? I recognize that You're the all-knowing, all-seeing God, and You have full understanding of what this situation needs. Remind me of this truth when I'm tempted to lean on my own knowledge. Ground me in Your Word so I'm equipped for the decision ahead.

When voices and opinions clamor in my mind, settle me down to process what's needed. I know I can't think clearly when worry is present, so I pray for peace and vision to see what You're asking of me. If I need to seek counsel from others, please show me where to turn. Help me reach out to those who have made a similar decision, and surround me with experts who can offer clarity and guidance. In all my interactions, give me the right questions to ask and a listening ear.

As I sift through information, keep my heart open to Your leading. Whatever is required, I pray for willpower to follow through and the words to communicate to my care recipient in a way that's understood and accepted.

Thank You for indwelling me with Your Spirit of wisdom. What a comfort to know I don't have to make this decision alone. I place it in Your hands and trust You to lead me.

In Jesus's name, amen.

14

When You Miss Home

For those whose caregiving requires time
away from home.

*How lovely is your dwelling place, LORD Almighty! My soul
yearns, even faints, for the courts of the LORD; my heart and
my flesh cry out for the living God.*

PSALM 84:1-2

———

Everywhere you look, the familiar is out of reach. Perhaps you're sleeping on a pullout couch and long
for the softness of your own bed. Maybe you're tired of
eating cafeteria food and crave a home-cooked meal.
Maybe it's the people at home you miss while you're
called away to care for someone else.

Dear friend, no matter your location or time away
from home, I pray you'll find rest in the presence of
Jesus. Scripture says He offers a safe place for you to

dwell. One Bible translation says, "My soul yearns, yes, even pines and is homesick for the courts of the Lord" (Psalm 84:2 AMPC).

You likely know homesickness very well right now. You long for familiar sights, sounds, and people. But even if your physical location doesn't change, God can ease your homesickness with His love. He is living and active here in this moment, longing to give the comfort you need.

Will you let Him?

―⁓―

Dear Lord,

I feel so torn as I provide care away from home. I know I'm where I need to be, but sometimes it feels as though I'm wandering through a foreign land. I'm surrounded by unfamiliar sights, smells, and sounds. Even the language is foreign at times, with medical jargon being spoken by hospital staff or different TV stations being chosen by my care recipient. I just want to relax again.

Lord, I'm thankful that as I face the unfamiliar, You offer a home within these walls. Your presence knows no limits, and Your comfort is available to me wherever

I am. Whether a change in scenery is on the horizon or not, I ask for an awareness of Your working here and now.

Show me ways I can keep the familiar nearby, whether bringing a favorite blanket or having access to a kitchen for home-cooked food. I recognize my care recipient may also struggle with homesickness, especially if we're at a medical facility for a while. Help me remain aware of her needs during this time. If I can bring comfort to both of us, please reveal that to me.

Your Word has such strong imagery for what I'm feeling right now. I confess I get so insulated in my struggle that I fail to recognize the deeper soul longing for You—the yearning of a heart that can only find peace in Your presence.

I cry out to You now, Lord. I believe You are living and active in my life, and I seek my shelter in You alone. Thank You for providing a safe dwelling. I lean into You and accept Your gift of peace.

In Jesus's name, amen.

15

When You Need a Second Opinion

For those who need additional guidance for someone under their care.

The fear of the LORD is the beginning of wisdom; all who follow his precepts have good understanding. To him belongs eternal praise.

PSALM 111:10

———٪٪٪———

Pressure bears down on you as treatment options fill your agenda. Making decisions for someone's health is a heavy weight to carry. If you lack a medical background, the burden is even heavier.

As you process advice from doctors, you might question where to go from here. Perhaps you're not sure you agree with their decision, but getting a second opinion brings its own challenges. What if you get conflicting answers? What if you lose time, and your care recipient's health suffers more? What if it means a move in location?

All these questions may leave you unsure, but remember you have an eternal God who offers unmatched wisdom. He invites you to soak in truth from His Word and seek Him in prayer. As you consider the options, He'll give you clarity and purpose to move forward.

This time of uncertainty may leave you anxious, but it can be an opportunity to draw close to God. He's ready to lead you where you need to go.

Will you listen and follow?

—⁓—

Dear Lord,

It's unsettling to realize I may need additional guidance for my care recipient. The advice we've received might be correct, but I sense we need a second opinion. So many new questions come with that decision, though. I worry that we may not receive clear answers, or the time delay could cause a setback in my care recipient's health. I also worry about finances and location. Can we handle another medical bill or move to a different facility?

As these thoughts race through my mind, I'm thankful You're a steady source of wisdom. You see everything happening in my care recipient's body, and You know what's best for him. I'm also grateful You've provided doctors and medical staff to help us through this. I may be unclear on where to turn, but You can lead us to the right team for what we need.

Keep me plugged in to Your Word, Lord, so I don't miss anything You might reveal to me. When I'm tempted to rely on my own understanding, draw me back to You in prayer. I don't want to move forward without considering all the options.

If there are people near me who can provide a reference or recommendation, would You help me see them? Give me wisdom as I weigh the different opinions. I want to consider everything, including the physical and emotional well-being of my care recipient, so I ask for a clear mind to work through all the scenarios.

As I move forward, I pray You would make Your presence known and felt. I believe You're a never-changing God, and I'm grateful You see what lies ahead. Guide me through each moment as I place my trust in You.

In Jesus's name, amen.

16

When You Need More Help

For those who need reinforcements in providing care.

*Two are better than one, because they have a good return
for their labor: If either of them falls down, one can help the
other up… Though one may be overpowered, two can defend
themselves. A cord of three strands is not quickly broken.*

ECCLESIASTES 4:9-10,12

You've given everything you have, and yet it's still not
enough. Not only do you feel stretched thin in this
role, but unfinished tasks linger at home too. As humbling as it is to admit, you've reached your capacity.

The next step may mean putting an aging parent into
a nursing home, or it may mean reaching out for help
to continue the current care plan. It may involve letting
go of extra commitments or seeking creative solutions
to get it all done.

However you choose to move forward, remember that God hasn't created you to do this alone. He places people in your life to come alongside you. Maybe they're longtime friends who have asked how they can help or acquaintances who have walked a similar road. Whomever God plants nearby, accept His invitation to find support.

You may reach your limits, but a "cord of three strands" will keep you strong.

Will you allow Him to help you now?

—⁓—

Dear Lord,

I've come to the realization I can't do it all. I wish I had the margin to handle what's in front of me, but the truth is, I don't. There's no way to move forward without finding someone else to help. It's a humbling place to be, and yet I know You can work in this situation. You're the Great Provider, and You'll supply what I need.

As I analyze my schedule, I ask for wisdom to see windows of possibility. Show me where things can be trimmed or removed, and give me resolve to follow through. If I need to change my care recipient's plan, help me consider the options with You as my guide.

I don't want to make hasty changes just to give myself relief, but I want to think through all the implications first.

I also pray for wisdom to see creative solutions. As I think through my calendar, reveal ways I can manage my time or complete tasks more efficiently. If there's a new skill I can learn to ease my schedule, equip me with what I need. I pray for clarity of mind to recognize the opportunities in front of me.

If there are people nearby who can help, would You open my eyes to see them? Whether old friends or new, I don't want to miss those You've placed in my life. I ask for protection and strength for my support system here and at home.

As I press through this exhausting time, remind me of Your presence each day. I'm limited in time and energy, but You have no limits. I want to loosen my grip so I can approach this season with grace. I acknowledge I can't do it all, and that's okay.

Fill me with clear perspective to move forward with confidence. As I evaluate and reach out for help, I trust You to be my strength.

In Jesus's name, amen.

17

When You Need Someone to Comfort *You*

For those who need a shoulder to cry on.

I am worn out from sobbing. All night I flood my bed with weeping, drenching it with my tears. My vision is blurred by grief; my eyes are worn out because of all my enemies... The LORD has heard my plea; the LORD will answer my prayer.

PSALM 6:6-7,9 NLT

———

Day in and day out, you pour into the life of another. You clean messes, you reassure, you calm fears... and all the while you process the same difficulty and pain. You want to be strong for your care recipient, but the truth is, you're struggling too. Watching her suffer is far from easy, and you find your own fears and worries growing until they're ready to burst.

While you may not be able to express your emotion to everyone, you wonder if there's anyone out there who can handle it. A listening ear, a reassuring hug, a comforting word. Any of these would be a welcome salve for your hurting soul.

Dear friend, when emotion overwhelms you, remember that your heavenly Father is listening and sees. He surrounds you with His arms and gives you freedom to let it out. Your tears are welcome in His presence. He doesn't condemn you for your struggle. Instead, He welcomes it and offers His peace. He longs to meet you in this place and cover you with His love.

Will you lean into Him now?

—∞—

Dear Lord,

Emotion is sitting at the surface, ready to bubble over at any moment. I'm not sure when or where I can let it out. This role has caused me to see more heartache and pain than I'd like. Watching my care recipient suffer is far from easy, and I don't feel safe expressing my struggle since she has worries of her own. I waffle between trying to stay strong and barely holding it together.

As I struggle through these emotions, I'm thankful

You're here in the midst of my pain. My tears aren't a burden to You. In fact, You see each one. Fill me with awareness of Your presence in this moment. I want to feel Your comfort flowing over me like a gentle rain—soothing and cleansing as it washes my face.

If I need to reach out to someone for support—whether a pastor, counselor, or friend—enable me to seek the help I need. Bring people into my life who can share the burden and keep me strong.

Whether I have support from other people or not, I commit to coming to You as I am. You give me the freedom to bring every emotion, sorrow, and fear to You. My pain isn't hidden, and I'm so thankful for that. Help me remove the mask as I rest in Your presence. I lean into You now and trust You to soothe every care.

In Jesus's name, amen.

18

When You See No Way Out

For those who have lost their vision beyond
their current struggle.

*You, God, tested us; you refined us like silver. You
brought us into prison and laid burdens on our
backs. You let people ride over our heads; we went
through fire and water, but you brought us to a
place of abundance.*

PSALM 66:10-12

———

Trapped is the perfect word to describe how you feel
right now. Your work continues day after day, and
no relief is in sight.

Maybe your care recipient faces a long-term health
challenge, such as paralysis or chronic pain. Perhaps
you're providing care away from home, and it doesn't
look as if your location will change anytime soon.

Maybe you simply feel stuck in the problems of today and can't imagine life will ever improve.

My friend, as you drown in these thoughts, I pray you'll find comfort in God's presence. Scripture says hardships will come. Burdens will be laid on your back. People will trample over you. You'll have to go through fire and water. But a place of abundance awaits.

Just as silver has to go through intense heat in order to shine, you, too, are a precious metal being refined. You may struggle to see how God could take this painful season and turn it into good, but He's working behind the scenes, creating a masterpiece. Whatever the situation, He can take your despair and turn it into hope.

Will you allow Him to do that?

—⁓—

Dear Lord,

I wish I were coming to you with unwavering faith, but the truth is, I am struggling. This season of caregiving seems endless, and I don't know how it could ever improve. Not only am I battling exhaustion and frayed emotions, but I want to stay strong for my care recipient too. I know I can't continue like this forever, but I don't see a way out.

Even though I feel caught in the middle of a dark tunnel, I know if I keep putting one foot in front of the other, sunlight *will* peek through. Would You show me a glimpse of that light now?

As I wade through my doubts and despair, I want to cling to the truth of who You are. It's not easy to read Scripture passages that talk about suffering. You don't promise a problem-free life, but You do promise to work all things for good. As much as I want to see the full picture, I ask for faith to trust Your plan. When I'm weighed down by my burdens, remind me they aren't mine to carry. You take every step by my side, and Your strength and peace will sustain me.

If You can use this season to refine me, I offer my heart with open hands. I may not like the painful moments ahead, but I believe You can turn them into a masterpiece of praise. I surrender to Your plan and choose to trust You.

In Jesus's name, amen.

19

When You Want a Moment to Yourself

For those who need time alone.

The news about [Jesus] spread all the more, so that crowds of people came to hear him and to be healed of their sicknesses. But Jesus often withdrew to lonely places and prayed.

——◊◊◊——

No matter where you turn, noise and conversation disrupt your longing for quiet. Perhaps you're with your care recipient in the hospital, and nurses visit every couple hours to do their tasks. Maybe a steady stream of well-wishers comes and goes, and you're the one who answers their questions. Perhaps your care recipient can't function on his own, leaving you tethered to his side. As much as you want to be kind, you just need some time to yourself.

Moments of solitude may elude you, but I pray you're comforted by the fact that Jesus faced this struggle too. In His ministry on earth, people crowded around Him, wanting to hear what He had to say, longing to be touched by His healing hand.

Yet even as the crowds closed in, He withdrew to quiet places to pray. It doesn't seem very loving, does it? The Son of God ignoring the needs around Him? But perhaps His separation was the most loving thing He could do because it allowed Him to draw from His Father's strength.

As you face the needs around you, remember that the Creator offers you His strength too. He's waiting to meet you where you are so He can provide a place of quiet rest.

Will you accept His invitation?

—*w*—

Dear Lord,

I'll admit I'm worn out from being around other people. I know it sounds selfish—as if I don't want to help my care recipient or respond to people who visit. But the truth is, I'm drained dry. Life before caregiving was so different. It wasn't always easy, but I could find moments to be alone. Now it seems as though I'm on call to meet everyone's needs and answer every question.

Lord, as I face this desire for time alone, I'm so grateful You understand my struggle. Your Son Jesus was in high demand during His earthly ministry, but He intentionally withdrew to be in Your presence. What a wonderful example of seeking You first.

It's hard to see opportunities when I can come to You in prayer, but I ask for them to open. Give me a willing spirit to take advantage of the moments You provide. Sometimes I'm tempted to spend my solitude in mindless pursuits. I know they can be a healthy way to unwind, but I don't want them to come at the expense of being with You. I need You every moment of this journey, so I ask You to fill me with the desire to seek You first.

When interruptions do come, I ask for Your grace to fill me. I don't want to hurt others with words of frustration. Show me how to respond in a respectful, God-honoring way. If I'm enabling someone to take advantage of me, especially my care recipient, I ask for courage to build healthy boundaries and the ability to communicate with love.

Father, thank You for always being here. You're a safe place of rest, offering peace in the midst of this noisy world. I come to You now and trust You to refill me.

In Jesus's name, amen.

20

When You Watch Your Care Recipient Go into Surgery

For those who are sending someone into
the operating room.

We wait in hope for the LORD; he is our help and our shield.
In him our hearts rejoice, for we trust in his holy name.
May your unfailing love be with us, LORD,
even as we put our hope in you.

PSALM 33:20-22

———

Helplessness washes over you as your care recipient is wheeled off to the operating room. You give one last hug, one last word of assurance. But deep inside, you wonder if you'll see her again.

Your loved one may be going into serious surgery, with life on the line. Or she may be headed into a routine procedure that doesn't seem threatening, but you know nothing is guaranteed. As you sit in the waiting room, fear may spiral through you. You're eager for a report, but you want the medical staff to do the job right. If the wait is long, you may alternate between worry and exhaustion.

Wherever you find yourself, I pray you'll seek refuge in God. He's watching over the operating room, and He's here with you as you wait. When anxiety mounts, He'll cover you with His love. He's a good God—a help and shield and a source of hope. It may feel impossible to settle into a place of trust, but He promises to turn your cares into a deep, abiding joy.

Will you let Him do that now?

—◊◊◊—

Dear Lord,

I feel helpless acknowledging that my care recipient's health is hanging in the balance. Whether her procedure is life threatening or not, I know anything can happen. I also know I can't stay in this place of worry forever.

No matter what comes, I'm so grateful for the reminder that You're in all places at all times. You're in the operating room, and You're here with me now. Please remind me of this when I forget. As I pass the time, I want to turn every worry into a prayer—to not let concerns fester, but to breathe them directly to You.

I believe You're a loving God who offers help and strength. As the minutes pass, I ask for Your presence to dwell among those in the operating room. Fill the doctors with wisdom, and guide their movements with precision and skill. I lift in prayer the medical team around them and ask for a sense of unity and purpose in their work. If problems arise, keep them levelheaded and give them swift reflexes to navigate the challenges. I pray You would work through them for a successful outcome, and I choose to trust You no matter what happens.

As I spend this time waiting, I ask for open eyes to see those around me. So many needs fill this building, and each person represents a soul You fashioned and formed. As our paths cross, help me be an ambassador of Your love. Even though I face my own worries, You've offered me hope in the Bible. Would You allow me to share that hope with someone else today?

Thank You for filling me with joy in the midst of uncertainty. I place these next hours in Your hands and trust Your plan.

In Jesus's name, amen.

21

When Your Care Recipient Doesn't Act like Himself

For those whose care recipient behaves
out of character.

*Love endures with patience and serenity, love is
kind and thoughtful, and is not jealous or envious;
love does not brag and is not proud or arrogant. It
is not rude; it is not self-seeking, it is not provoked
[nor overly sensitive and easily angered]; it does
not take into account a wrong endured. It does
not rejoice at injustice, but rejoices with the truth
[when right and truth prevail]. Love bears all
things [regardless of what comes], believes all
things [looking for the best in each one], hopes all
things [remaining steadfast during difficult times],
endures all things [without weakening].*

1 CORINTHIANS 13:4-7 AMP

—~~~—

You see your care recipient—a person you've known and loved—but it seems as though someone else has invaded his body. Maybe he's fighting a mental illness that's changed who he is and what he remembers. Perhaps medication has altered his behavior. Or maybe he's weary or fearful of his condition and takes it out on whoever is nearby.

Regardless of the cause, you're struggling to stay level-headed. An extra measure of patience is needed, but you feel tapped out. If you've known your care recipient for many years, you might grieve the person he used to be.

Dear friend, while you care for someone who seems like a stranger, remember you have a refuge in God. He offers a love that is patient and kind. It endures every challenge, seeks the best in every person, and remains steadfast in every storm. This gift is available to you right now.

When you battle impatience, frustration, or grief, let your heavenly Father's love pour through you. He can fill every gap and meet every need.

Will you turn to Him now?

—∞—

Dear Lord,

It's so hard to watch my care recipient's behavior and wish we could rewind time. This condition has changed him in many ways, and I long to return to normal. Whether it's hurtful words or a memory that's been stolen by disease, I often feel the brunt of his actions. Will this situation ever feel stable again?

Father, as I yearn for glimpses of my care recipient's former self, I'm thankful You never change. You're a God of immense love that extends beyond the emotions of this world. Even now, You're filling me with that love. Would You reveal how I can share it with my care recipient?

When I'm tempted to lash out in harmful ways, I ask You to bring me in check. This situation isn't easy, but I don't want to make it harder by releasing my frustration on others. I know You're a safe sounding board, and I choose to turn to You first when I face a challenge.

Help me view these moments as opportunities to build a bridge with my care recipient. Whether he's aware of his actions or not, I know You can fill me with love. Help me respond in a way that isn't overly sensitive or easily angered, but that's selfless, patient, and forgiving. You're the only One who can change my perspective, and I place my hope and trust in You.

In Jesus's name, amen.

22

When Your Care Recipient Ignores Medical Instructions

For those who feel the brunt of someone
else's poor choices.

*Be wise in the way you act toward outsiders; make the most
of every opportunity. Let your conversation be always full
of grace, seasoned with salt, so that you may know how to
answer everyone.*

COLOSSIANS 4:5-6

———

Your care recipient has done it again. Whether inten-
tional or not, she's disregarded doctors' orders and
charted her own course. Now you're left to pick up the
pieces and answer for her actions. If only you could
change her choice, but it's impossible.

A myriad of emotions may rush in. You might be
frustrated or angry that she hasn't done what's expected.

Perhaps you worry her actions will cause more harm. Maybe you dread the conversation you need to have next, whether with your care recipient or her medical team.

Wherever you find yourself, I pray you'll draw strength from the ultimate Grace Giver. When you feel inadequate for the task ahead, He'll help you see your care recipient through His eyes. She may put you in a tough position, but God will guide the way. He can turn this challenge into an opportunity and fill you with wisdom.

Will you seek Him now?

—⁂—

Dear Lord,

It's so frustrating to be put in the position of having to answer for someone else's actions. I find myself waffling between impatience, anger, dread, and guilt. Sometimes I wonder if I missed the mark and caused this to happen. Other times I place the blame at my care recipient's feet. I don't want anything to set us back, and these choices do just that.

Lord, no matter what emotion fills me in this moment, I'm grateful You're a steady rock. You see my struggle and promise to guide me. Thank You for extending unmatched grace. Even though my frustration is aimed at someone else, I know I'm not perfect either. You love and forgive me when my sin deserves so much worse.

Would You flood me with that same grace right now? If I need to confront my care recipient about her behavior, enable me to do so with Your Spirit's leading. Soothe any anger and soften my bitterness. If I've responded to her in hurtful ways, give me humility to make it right. Even if reconciliation doesn't come, allow me to rest in the knowledge that I've shown Your love.

When I'm asked to answer to medical staff for my care recipient's actions, I pray for the right words. I want to give an honest explanation, but I also don't want to dishonor someone close to me. If an adjustment is needed in treatment, may this be a time of clarity as we explore the options.

Whether changes are made or not, I come to You for everything I need. You offer immeasurable grace and wisdom, and I trust You to guide me now.

In Jesus's name, amen.

23

When Your Care Recipient Is Admitted to the Hospital

For those supporting someone through focused medical care.

Have I not commanded you? Be strong and courageous.
Do not be afraid; do not be discouraged, for the LORD
your God will be with you wherever you go.

JOSHUA 1:9

———— ∽ ————

Ready or not, a change in scenery has arrived. Your care recipient's health has worsened, and now he's in the hospital.

You may find yourself bombarded with emotions in this new season. Maybe you're relieved you don't have to shoulder the caregiving burden alone. Perhaps a sliver of worry has embedded itself in your mind. Maybe exhaustion weighs you down as you find yourself pulled in yet another direction.

Whatever comes, my friend, remember that God will supply what you need. As you provide care in a different environment or face new worries, your heavenly Father is here with you. He can take this situation and work all things for good. He sees what lies ahead and is making a way.

When fear and discouragement wrestle inside you, turn to the One who can breathe new life. He offers strength to those who seek Him.

Will you let Him help you now?

—✺—

Dear Lord,

So many thoughts race through my mind as I face the days ahead with my care recipient. It feels as if our world has tipped sideways, and I'm scrambling to stay upright and hold it all together. Not only do I have questions and worry, but I'm also called upon by others to provide answers—all while juggling new logistics and care needs.

This situation has reminded me that I can't walk through life without You. I'm so grateful nothing takes

You by surprise. You knew this was coming, and You've remained by my side.

Thank You for providing the medical care that's needed right now. As doctors evaluate my care recipient's condition, I pray You would help them see any trouble spots and recognize the right treatment. If I'm asked to provide context of the situation, help me communicate clearly so the best plan can be made.

As I balance my time here and at home, I ask for an extra measure of strength. My to-do list is overwhelming, but You can fill in the gaps. Give me wisdom as I evaluate priorities, and enable me to release commitments that aren't urgent. If I need to reach out for help, please show me who's nearby and allow me to communicate the need.

Whether this hospitalization brings healing to my care recipient or not, I choose to trust You. The coming days may be filled with fear and discouragement, but You are with me. I lean into Your mighty hand to help me through this time.

In Jesus's name, amen.

24

When Your Care Recipient Is Depressed

For those struggling to stay above the cloud of someone else's depression.

Why, my soul, are you downcast?
Why so disturbed within me?
Put your hope in God, for I will yet praise him,
my Savior and my God.

PSALM 42:5

—∿—

You don't want to get dragged down, but there are times when you can't help it. Navigating illness with someone isn't easy, but when she's battling depression, the struggle intensifies.

Perhaps you've done everything you can to remain positive, but one sentence from your care recipient lowers the mood again. Maybe her sad silence hovers in the room, speaking louder than words ever could. However the depression manifests itself, it can seep into your soul and steal your joy.

Dear friend, rest assured this struggle is normal and your Father is here to help. Just as the psalmist admitted to feeling downcast, you can be honest with God about your struggle too. He doesn't judge or expect a false happy front. He accepts you as you are.

You may feel the world's weight pressing in on you, but keep holding on. God can meet you in this hard place and fill you with hope.

Will you look to Him now?

———

Dear Lord,

Working with someone who's depressed is harder than I anticipated. It's as if a black cloud looms over my care recipient, and it has blanketed everyone around her. I try to stay positive—to get away from the darkness—but it's unrelenting. Is there any relief in sight?

Father, when I struggle to see signs of hope, I'm grateful You welcome me as I am. The Bible says Your "light shines on in the darkness" (John 1:5 AMP). It doesn't say the darkness is a figment of my imagination, but that

You're present in the midst of it. Thank You for meeting me here right now.

As I struggle to escape this cloud, I want to see glimpses of You. Would You open my eyes to recognize how You're moving in my circumstances? Give me a hunger to read Your Word and allow its truth to wash over me.

I also ask for the right words as I interact with my care recipient. I don't want to minimize her trial in any way, because I know it's immense. But I do want to be a messenger of hope, shining Your light in her dark world.

If her depression can be helped by a change in scenery or activity, please reveal it to me and help me suggest it in a way that will be well received. If she needs help for her depression beyond what I can give, grant me wisdom to recognize that. I don't want to ignore warning signs in my care recipient or myself, so I trust You to guide us.

Lord, whether the cloud lifts or not, I come to You for the hope I need. I believe You're here with me now, and I look to You as my sole source of joy.

In Jesus's name, amen.

25

When Your Care Recipient Is in Pain

For those helping someone who is physically hurting.

May the Lord of peace Himself grant you His peace at all times and in every way [that peace and spiritual well-being that comes to those who walk with Him, regardless of life's circumstances]. The Lord be with you all.

2 THESSALONIANS 3:16 AMP

———※———

You stand by and watch as your care recipient grimaces in pain. You've tried everything to help, but there's only so much you can do. Perhaps you long to take his place—to remove his burden and put it on yourself. Instead, you're left to worry on the sidelines. Maybe it's too hard to witness his struggle, but you can't leave him alone. No matter what you do, you feel trapped in a no-win scenario.

My friend, while this situation seems helpless, remember that God has placed you here for a purpose. He sees everything and promises to be with you. When you're filled with angst, He offers a deep well of peace for your soul.

Even if you can't remove your care recipient's pain, your heavenly Father can use you to administer His peace. He calls you to seek what you need in Him.

Will you do that now?

—⁂—

Dear Lord,

I'll admit I'm struggling as I watch my care recipient. It doesn't seem fair that he has to suffer like this. I wish I could make it all go away—to return to normal life and turn this trial into a distant memory. I long for relief, but it isn't anywhere on the horizon.

As I sag under the weight of this helplessness, Lord, I'm thankful You're here with me. You see the struggle, and You feel my care recipient's pain. So much about this situation isn't peaceful. Grimaces, groans, and cries break the silence. Adjustments to medication seem never ending. And yet amid the suffering, You remain present.

Thank You for providing what's needed in this hardship. As I move forward, I ask for wisdom to follow the right treatment plan for my care recipient. If his environment can be changed to bring more comfort, show me those opportunities. If further medical help is needed, I pray for clarity to recognize that.

When his pain flares, please keep my heart and mind calm. You offer peace that transcends the circumstances of this world, and I want it to fill me now. Draw me to Your side when I feel on edge, and allow Your Spirit to flow through me so I can offer comfort to my care recipient.

I believe You can ease his physical pain, and I ask You to do that if it's in Your will. But if You choose to keep us here, I commit to trusting Your plan. Whatever comes, I lift my eyes above this hardship and rest in You.

In Jesus's name, amen.

26

When Your Care Recipient Is Mistreated

For those supporting someone through
mistreatment by medical staff.

*You have heard that it was said, "Love your neighbor
and hate your enemy." But I tell you, love your enemies
and pray for those who persecute you, that you may be
children of your Father in heaven.*

MATTHEW 5:43-45

———

Anger pulses through you as you watch your care
recipient suffer at the hand of someone else. Perhaps a doctor makes a careless comment in an appoint-
ment. An aide might be gruff as he goes about his duties.
Maybe a nurse is harsh with her words or actions. These
scenarios and more leave you seeking justice as the

primary caregiver, your cause rising up inside until it threatens to boil over.

My friend, while you can't control the actions of others, I pray you're inspired by Jesus's example of selfless love. Countless times in His earthly ministry, He faced ridicule and persecution. He didn't turn His head to injustice, but He kept His heart tuned to His Father in prayer.

Your situation may tempt you to lash out at others, but take a moment to sit in God's presence. As He calms you, He can help you move forward with grace. His love and forgiveness are available to everyone, and He longs to share them through you now.

Will you let Him?

—⁓—

Dear Lord,

It seems impossible to stay levelheaded right now. As if this situation isn't hard already, the carelessness of others has added to the wounds. Can't they see my care recipient is suffering enough? I feel caught in the middle, trying to make things right and assure my care recipient she'll be okay.

I'll admit I struggle to view the offender through Your eyes, but I know You can help me. When a lack of forgiveness strangles my spirit, would You loosen its grip with Your love? The last thing I want to do is pray for someone who has hurt those close to me—the frustration is too raw—but I know You call me to do that. Help me trust in Your ways, and soften my heart to see everyone as Your creation, deserving of forgiveness.

If I need to take steps to confront behavior, fill me with wisdom to say the right thing. I can't ignore injustice, but I also want to move forward in a way that honors You.

As my care recipient struggles in the wake of mistreatment, help me be a solid support to her. I don't want my anger and bitterness to spread, so I bring them to You and allow You to mold me. It's impossible to reverse time, but I trust You can meet both of us here, providing comfort and help. I turn to You now and choose to follow Your lead.

In Jesus's name, amen.

27

When Your Care Recipient Won't Let You Help

For those whose care recipient insists on taking care of himself.

Since God chose you to be the holy people he loves, you must clothe yourselves with tenderhearted mercy, kindness, humility, gentleness, and patience.

COLOSSIANS 3:12 NLT

———

Your care recipient has that look in his eye. He's taken the word *independence* to a new level, and you've found yourself in a battle.

You know his medical restrictions and limits, but he isn't heeding them. A stubborn will has taken over, and he's pushing you away. Frustration grows as you try to draw healthy boundaries. Is there any way to do your job and keep him from further harm?

My friend, when your care recipient tests every limit, remember that your heavenly Father offers a boundless love. He has chosen you not only to be His child, but to provide care in this situation. When He calls you to live in "tenderhearted mercy, kindness, humility, gentleness, and patience," He doesn't leave you to drum up those traits within yourself. Instead, He offers an unending supply.

One translation of Scripture defines patience as "the power to endure whatever injustice or unpleasantness comes, with good temper" (Colossians 3:12 AMP). You may feel far from good tempered, and your relationship with your care recipient may be anything but pleasant, but you can always turn to the One who will help you through.

Will you call on Him now?

—m—

Dear Lord,

I hate feeling frustrated with my care recipient, but it's a challenge to get him to cooperate. I'm not trying to be overbearing in my care, yet he continually pushes me away. I worry about his long-term health if he insists on stepping outside the bounds of his condition. Not only that, but the strain on our relationship has become a challenge.

Father, as I respond to this situation, would You keep me focused on You? I want to do the right thing as I offer care, and some of these moments aren't black and white. If I'm enforcing help in areas where my care recipient is capable, allow me to see that. I know independence is important to him, and I don't want to squelch it unnecessarily. Fill me with humility to admit when I've erred.

If he's harming himself through his actions, give me strength to redirect him. The last thing I want is to bottle my frustration or let it spill out in stinging words, so draw me close to You when I'm tempted. If I need further help in enforcing his care, show me where to seek it.

Most of all, I ask for Your mercy, kindness, gentleness, and patience to flood me. I know those traits don't always come naturally, but they're available in You. Turn my mind to You in moments of frustration, and let Your heart of compassion flow through me.

In Jesus's name, amen.

28

When Your Faith Is Gone

For those who have lost their hope in God.

My tears have been my food day and night,
while people say to me all day long, "Where is your God?"

PSALM 42:3

[Jesus] replied, "If you have faith as small as a mustard seed,
you can say to this mulberry tree, 'Be uprooted and planted
in the sea,' and it will obey you."

LUKE 17:6

———∞———

W here is God?"

Have you found yourself asking that question? Whether you're a new believer or you've gone to church your whole life, watching someone else's pain tests what you know about your Savior. Perhaps you question why He would allow this to happen or why He won't do anything to fix it.

Verses such as Luke 17:6 may be quoted to you, but deep inside you don't believe them. You've been clinging to your faith, but you haven't seen any trees move. It's as if God has abandoned the premises and left you to do the heavy lifting yourself.

Dear friend, you may barely be holding on to your faith, but know that the Lord is still here. When you seek His will, He promises to provide what you need. It may look different than what you want, but He's faithful to move on your behalf. Even if everything else in this world disappoints, God longs to draw you close to Himself in relationship. He's always present, ready to take your mustard seed of faith and grow new life within you.

Will you turn to Him now?

—⁓—

Dear Lord,

It seems weird talking to a God I don't trust, but here I am. This situation is so bleak that it's hard to see any sign of Your presence. Whether it's the pain of watching my care recipient suffer or exhaustion from everything required of me, I find myself questioning if You care. It's as if every ounce of faith has been squeezed out of me until there are no drops left.

While part of me wants to hold on to my hurt, I also recognize I can't dwell here. I may be trapped in this situation, but I don't have to live in bitterness and defeat. When they threaten to consume me, would You turn my gaze to You? Give me courage to come to You whenever I doubt—to be honest rather than trying to hide. I know You hear my thoughts, so I bring each one to You.

As I grapple with questions of faith, please guide me to the right resources and people who can help. The world offers a million answers, but the only source of truth is Your Word. Help me seek my answers in Scripture and filter advice through Your lens.

Although I struggle to see You working, I want to be filled with hope again. I pray for glimpses of Your presence so I can see You moving here and now. I choose to trust You, even when I don't understand, and I ask You to grow this seed of faith within me.

In Jesus's name, amen.

29

When Your Other Relationships Are Suffering

For those with relationships barely holding together.

We don't yet see things clearly. We're squinting in a fog, peering through a mist. But it won't be long before the weather clears and the sun shines bright! We'll see it all then, see it all as clearly as God sees us, knowing him directly just as he knows us! But for right now, until that completeness, we have three things to do to lead us toward that consummation: Trust steadily in God, hope unswervingly, love extravagantly. And the best of the three is love.

1 CORINTHIANS 13:12-13 MSG

⎯⎯⎯⎯

While you pour into the life of another, so many relationships feel as if they're on life support. Demands on your time take you away from home. Physical needs leave you exhausted. Your emotions and spirit are on edge, and the closest outlet is the people near you—spouse, children, or friends. All of these links become more frayed until you fear they'll snap.

My friend, your relationships may barely be holding on, but there is One who offers a safe place to land. As distance mounts, He draws you close. You may struggle to glimpse beyond today, but God sees and knows.

Even now, He can work within you to renew your hope. He may not reveal the whole picture, but He calls you to a life of extravagant love. In fact, He wants you to prioritize it above all else. When caregiving pulls you from other relationships, lean into the ultimate Source of what you need. He can pour through you and restore what's been broken.

Will you let Him do that now?

—— ⁓⁓ ——

Dear Lord,

This fracture in my relationships has taken a toll. It feels as if caregiving has stretched us apart like a rubber band. Every hurtful word or hour apart pulls the band tighter, and it's just a matter of time before it snaps. I'm so exhausted from my tasks that it feels like too much work to communicate with others, but I know I can't ignore this distance forever.

As I seek to strengthen these relationships, would You guide me with Your love? I'm so grateful that when I struggle to see through the fog, You're working for my good. Thank You for offering a steady foundation to place my trust.

Even though this role takes me away from those close to me, I want to repair what's been broken. Please show me pockets of time when I can be with family and close friends. May we use that time to build each other up rather than flinging hurtful words or sitting in bitter silence. If I need to make amends, fill me with humility to right my wrongs. If further help is needed to bridge the gap, guide us to the right counselor or resource to move us forward.

I pray for physical and mental strength so I can be fully present with my family and friends. Caregiving drains so much out of me, but I know You can refill me with Your love. As I allow You to work in my heart, I trust You to restore my relationships and renew my hope.

In Jesus's name, amen.

30

When You're Burnt Out

For those who have nothing left to give.

Don't let the floods overwhelm me, or the deep waters swallow me, or the pit of death devour me. Answer my prayers, O LORD, for your unfailing love is wonderful. Take care of me, for your mercy is so plentiful.

PSALM 69:15-16 NLT

—⁂—

One minute you feel up to the task in front of you, but the next you feel spent. Whether strength has left you in a giant rush or a slow leak, you have nothing left to give. Tasks pile on top of each other, and you tell yourself you don't have time to rest. At the same time, you'll collapse if you don't stop. How can you care for someone when you're depleted?

Dear friend, in this season of exhaustion, don't forget your heavenly Father is here with you right now. When you're overwhelmed, He'll protect you from the flood. When you're drowning, He'll lift you to dry ground.

God cares for you with a love that never fails. Your body and emotions may wear out, but He won't. He's full of mercy and compassion, always listening to your prayers.

Will you reach out to Him now?

———

Dear Lord,

I come to You weak and empty. Caregiving has taken all I have to give, and yet it continues to ask for more. Not only is my body weary, but my mind is frazzled and my spirit is dry. Emotions hover at the surface sometimes, ready to escape, while other times they're stuffed so deep inside that I feel numb. I can only run on fumes for so long.

In the midst of my exhaustion, Lord, I'm thankful that You promise to never let me drown. This situation is far from easy, but You offer strength for the tasks ahead. When I reach my limits, You give me new energy and perspective to move forward.

Whenever I'm tempted to forget, would You bring me back? Draw me to You so I can be renewed in Your presence. I'm fully aware of my shortcomings, and I worry about keeping up with my care recipient's needs. I ask You to make Your power known in my weakness. Fill in the gaps with what's needed, and allow me to rest in the knowledge that You're overseeing each moment.

If I'm holding too tightly to my to-do list, loosen my grip so I can rest in Your grace. Thank You that You don't measure my worth by how much I accomplish, but my worth is grounded in who I am in You. You call me Your child—a creation of the Lord Almighty (2 Corinthians 6:18). That's an honor I don't want to neglect.

When I'm buried under tasks, remind me of Your unfailing love. It offers a sweet retreat and a place of comfort. Help me release my burdens and rest there now.

If I'm given small snatches of time alone, allow me to use the minutes wisely and turn to You for what I need. I trust that You can strengthen me for whatever comes. Your compassion far exceeds my limits, and Your mercy will see me through.

In Jesus's name, amen.

31

When You're Caught by Surprise

For those facing an unexpected health scare
with someone in their care.

*Don't fret or worry. Instead of worrying, pray. Let petitions
and praises shape your worries into prayers, letting God
know your concerns. Before you know it, a sense of God's
wholeness, everything coming together for good, will come
and settle you down. It's wonderful what happens when
Christ displaces worry at the center of your life.*

PHILIPPIANS 4:6-7 MSG

—∿—

It can happen in an instant. Life is rolling along—just
business as usual—until the phone rings, a diagnosis
hits, or an emergency sends you scrambling to help someone in your care. Health challenges are hard to navigate
in any circumstance, but when they catch you by surprise, your heart and mind are left to pick up the pieces.

Whether you're in the midst of the storm right now or coping with its aftermath, remember that your worries can always be shaped into prayers. You may feel helpless to provide what's needed, but you can call out to God. Your words don't have to be fancy or rehearsed. Just offer what you have and trust that He's listening.

He promises to turn your fears into a peace that makes no sense to the human mind. A peace that transcends the struggles of the moment. A peace that passes understanding.

Will you bring your cares to Him?

—— ᵐ ——

Dear Lord,

My emotions are reeling right now. As I struggle to wrap my brain around this situation, I can't help but look at the worst-case scenario and drown in fear. I know I need to have faith that You're here with me, but it's hard to keep my vision when I feel caught in a whirlwind. I want to stay calm for my care recipient too since she's facing fears of her own.

Even though I don't know what's ahead, would you fill me with an awareness of Your presence? Where worry is crowding out reason, remind me You're never caught by surprise. I may not know how the story will end, but You do.

Strengthen my faith to trust You regardless of the outcome. If this situation leads to more pain, I want to live in the peace only You provide. Help me draw my strength from You so I can be a solid support for those who need me. I pray You will keep my mind clear as I answer questions and soothe others' fears.

If my role changes as a result of this crisis, I ask You to equip me for whatever lies ahead. When I feel alone and scared, remind me You're a firm foundation, ever present and listening.

Thank You for watching over me. As I scramble to tie up loose ends in response to this emergency, remind me of Your love often. Show me what it looks like to lean on You. I release my fear into Your hands and trust You as my strength and support.

In Jesus's name, amen.

32

When You're Lonely

For those who want company while
caring for someone else.

The LORD is my shepherd; I have all that I need.
He lets me rest in green meadows;
he leads me beside peaceful streams. He renews my strength.

PSALM 23:1-3 NLT

———ᘰ———

The room ticks with silence as you find yourself
alone. Maybe you're sitting in a hospital waiting
room while your care recipient undergoes tests. Perhaps you're cooped up at home since his condition pre-
vents you from going anywhere. Maybe you're in a place
abounding with noise, but no one notices you as they
go about their day.

Whatever the source of your loneliness, I pray you'll
find refuge in God. No thought or emotion is hidden

from His sight. He sees your struggle and feels the ache in your soul. When other voices fall quiet, He's still with you, providing what you need.

Let this time of solitude renew your hope. As you seek His voice, He will lead and guide. As you rest in Him, He'll refresh and restore you. He's sitting with you in this very moment, offering companionship and a listening ear.

Will you lean on Him?

—⁓—

Dear Lord,

I know solitude can be a blessing, but lately it's made this situation harder. I face so many challenges, and there are countless moments spent alone. Sometimes I just want someone to share with. Even when my care recipient is nearby, I don't feel I can be open with him about every struggle.

As I face these moments, Lord, I'm grateful You're here with me now. I may long for human company, but Your presence soothes with a comfort that can't be matched on earth. When I wallow in loneliness, please open my eyes to see You in this place. You remain present, even though I feel left behind by everyone else.

If opportunities for new friendships present themselves, would You reveal them to me? I know I'm not the only one facing hardships, so I trust You to guide me to people who can form a circle of trust.

When my loneliness turns to boredom, show me how I can reach out to others with Your love. Various needs are all around me, and I don't want to become so insulated in my struggle that I fail to see them. Give me new energy and ideas, whether it's writing notes of encouragement or creating a support group.

Most of all, I ask You to make me more aware of Your presence. You offer rest and peace, and I look to You to fill the emptiness within me.

In Jesus's name, amen.

33

When You're Needed Somewhere Else

For those who feel torn between
multiple responsibilities.

*I lift up my eyes to the mountains—where does my help
come from? My help comes from the L*ORD*, the Maker of
heaven and earth. He will not let your foot slip—he who
watches over you will not slumber; indeed, he who watches
over Israel will neither slumber nor sleep.*

PSALM 121:1-4

—⟋⟍—

Y ou go about your tasks in one place, but your mind
is in another. Household, family, church, friends—
you fear you're letting them all down with your absence.
Perhaps you're taking a rare break from caregiving to do
something else, but you feel guilty for not being with your
care recipient. Wherever you go, it seems you can't win.

My friend, this tug-of-war may continue for a while, but God is ready to help. He made not only heaven and earth, but He also made *you*. He knows what overwhelms you, what lies ahead, and what you can handle. When it feels impossible to get it all done, He'll equip you to carry on. When you're exhausted, He'll give you rest.

Your Savior is always working on your behalf. You may feel trapped in a valley of never-ending tasks, but He calls you to lift your eyes to Him. He provides more than enough help to see you through.

Will you look to Him now?

—— ⁂ ——

Dear Lord,

I feel so torn as I face the demands around me. Caregiving requires a lot of my time, but life goes on outside these walls. My family needs me at home, my house needs to be cleaned, and other commitments call my name. No matter where I am or what I do, my mind flits to what needs to be done elsewhere. I wish I could clone myself so I would be able to do it all.

Lord, even though I'm overwhelmed at times, I'm grateful I don't have to tackle these tasks alone. You stand by my side and provide the strength I need. Thank You for being such a good God. You could have created me and left me to travel this world on my own, but You lovingly watch over me, making sure my feet don't slip.

As I go about my tasks, would You keep my eyes on You? Give me wisdom as I analyze my schedule, and show me where I can cut back. If there are commitments I'm holding on to selfishly, loosen my grip to release them. If I need to reach out for help, please lead me to the right resources and people. I don't want to take advantage of anyone, but I also know You've placed others in my life for a reason. Enable me to see those nearby who can step in, and give me a humble heart to ask for help.

When I worry about tasks elsewhere, remind me that You are an all-seeing God. You not only provide for me in this moment, but You're with those who feel my absence. This burden isn't mine to carry alone, so I release it to You and trust You to fill the void.

In Jesus's name, amen.

34

When You're Overwhelmed with Medical Instructions

For those who feel inadequate to follow someone else's care plan.

Trust GOD from the bottom of your heart; don't try to figure out everything on your own. Listen for God's voice in everything you do, everywhere you go; he's the one who will keep you on track.

PROVERBS 3:5-6 MSG

—⁂—

Instructions pile up, filed away in a brain on overload. Not only are you caring for someone's basic needs, but you have to decipher all the information too.

Maybe you're bringing a care recipient home from surgery, and you have a long list of medications to manage for her. Perhaps she has ongoing needs that require physical therapy at home, and her fill-in therapist is you.

Maybe a medical device has been attached to her—a heart pump, oxygen tank, or cast—and you're responsible to keep track of all the dos and don'ts.

Dear friend, you may feel inadequate for the tasks ahead, but remember you have a boundless supply of wisdom in your heavenly Father. He'll fill you with confidence when you're paralyzed by indecision. He'll give you the right questions when you need clarity. And He'll keep you on track when you make a wrong turn.

Whatever your void, He's willing and able to fill it. He longs for you to draw close and seek what you need in Him.

Will you do that now?

—⁓—

Dear Lord,

I'm facing a pile of instructions, and all I want to do is bury my head and go back to normal life. It's daunting to realize how much my care recipient needs. So many tasks are required—medication, physical therapy, changing dressings, or managing medical devices. Some of these could be life threatening if not executed properly, and the pressure is weighing on me.

Father, I'm grateful that when I feel inadequate, Your

voice breaks through the confusion. You speak in every situation and point the way. When I feel stuck, You can move me forward in trust.

I'll admit it's tempting to rely on my own knowledge. I'm grateful for the mind You've given me to process information, but I don't want to crowd You out. As I learn this new routine, please fill me with wisdom that can only come from You. If I need further understanding, give me the right questions to ask for a clear response. If I need assistance in implementing this routine, help me find the right resources.

I don't want to cause my care recipient more harm, and I recognize that an anxious spirit is prone to error. Keep my heart and mind calm as I follow instructions. When I'm overwhelmed by the big picture, focus my eyes on what's in front of me right now. Enable me to do the work I've been given and leave the rest in Your hands.

I'm so thankful You'll keep me on track no matter how bumpy the road gets. I trust You to guide me, and I lean on You for confidence and direction.

In Jesus's name, amen.

35

When You're Physically Exhausted

For those whose bodies are worn out.

The Holy Spirit helps us in our weakness. For example, we don't know what God wants us to pray for. But the Holy Spirit prays for us with groanings that cannot be expressed in words.

ROMANS 8:26 NLT

Your body drags as you put one foot in front of the other. Sometimes it's a challenge just to keep your head upright. So many tasks fill your to-do list, but when you're physically tired, they loom that much larger. All you want to do is rest, but it's not possible when you're on call to provide what your care recipient needs.

My friend, no matter how weary you feel right now,

remember you have an ever-present God whose strength knows no limits. He not only walks with you, but He *indwells* you, filling you when you're weak.

You may be so exhausted that thoughts won't form and words won't come, but your Father knows what you need. He'll fill in the gaps and speak on your behalf. Your physical strength may fade, but He can renew your spirit one prayer at a time.

Will you come to Him now?

------ɷɷ------

Dear Lord,

It's hard to put into words how weary I am. So much is required of me. Sometimes I feel like a sponge being wrung out day after day, with no chance to refill. Whether I'm helping my care recipient with physical tasks or getting by on less sleep, my body can only take so much.

I'm grateful for the reminder that I may reach my limits, but Your strength knows no bounds. You promise to sustain me and provide what I need. Would You do that right now? I long to feel Your presence flowing through me, so I open myself up to let You work.

If sleep isn't on the horizon, fill me with the energy I need to keep going. I don't want to get caught up in what tomorrow holds, so help me live in this moment, trusting You to carry me through. Revive my muscles and spirit for the tasks ahead. I believe You can work through me, even when I'm physically spent.

If I'm shouldering too much of the burden on my own, open my eyes to see that. I pray for clear communication with my care recipient and his other caregivers so we can draw healthy boundaries. If I need to adjust my schedule, I trust You to reveal the next steps. Give me discernment to know where You're leading and the willingness to obey.

When moments of rest do come, I ask You to soothe my mind with Your peace. Whatever worries or tasks may linger, let them float away as I close my eyes. Even if sleep only comes in short spurts, I believe You can provide a deep, rejuvenating slumber no matter the length of time.

Thank You for seeing my need and filling the gaps when I have nothing left to give. I entrust my body to Your care and ask You to work through my weakness.

In Jesus's name, amen.

36

When You're Scared of the Unknown

For those who are battling fear.

When I am afraid, I put my trust in you. In God, whose word I praise—in God I trust and am not afraid. What can mere mortals do to me?

PSALM 56:3-4

—⁓—

Fear has seized you and won't let go. A hundred scenarios lie before you, each one painting a future you don't want to experience.

Perhaps your care recipient has received a difficult diagnosis, and you dread what's in store. Maybe you read news stories that display evidence of this fallen world, and you pray they don't hit too close to home. Or maybe you look ahead to your care recipient's passing and wonder how you'll cope.

Whatever worries are swirling in your mind, trust that God knows each one. He sees beyond the struggles of today and has mapped out an eternal future. When anxiety threatens, He invites you to sit in His presence—to breathe in His peace.

His Word provides truth and light. As you turn to Him, He'll lift your eyes beyond this life to catch a glimpse of the next. Protection is yours, but even greater, He offers eternity in heaven. He's a trustworthy and praiseworthy Shield through this storm.

Will you put your hope in Him?

———

Dear Lord,

Anxiety has gripped me, and I can't seem to shake it. So many worries press in. *How will I get through this? What if I can't provide what's needed? What will I do when my care recipient dies?* They spin through my mind like a ribbon, tightening until I can't think straight.

Lord, even though I can't see past my fear, I believe You hold the future in Your hands, and You know what comes next. Thank You for accepting me as I am, fears and all. You don't require me to come to You with a perfect Christian facade, but You welcome my concerns and promise to meet each one. I come to You now, offering my feeble trust.

As I process these worries, would You draw me back to Your Word? I know the Bible is God breathed and offers hope for today. When I'm tempted to soothe my fear with temporary fixes, remind me of Your lasting peace. I want each concern to bounce right back to You in prayer.

If my care recipient is facing worries as well, I ask for wisdom to navigate them with her. Keep my eyes open to her needs, and help us lean on You. If she doesn't know You yet, give me the words to share Your gift of eternal salvation.

I recognize this world is full of pain and heartache, but it's not my ultimate destination. When anxiety threatens, turn my eyes to the promise of heaven. You are a trustworthy God—my Shield and Defender, my Prince of Peace. I place my fear in Your hands and lean on You.

In Jesus's name, amen.

37

When You're Tired of Keeping It All Together

For those who feel torn up inside but can't show it.

Save me, O God, for the waters have come up to my neck. I sink in the miry depths, where there is no foothold. I have come into the deep waters; the floods engulf me. I am worn out calling for help; my throat is parched. My eyes fail, looking for my God.

Psalm 69:1-3

The Lord hears the needy and does not despise his captive people.

Psalm 69:33

———

Emotions are stuffed down as each day passes. Worry, frustration, anger, heartache. These and so many more grow within you, but there's no way to release them. You're always on watch with your care recipient, and the last thing you want is to let him see the depth of your burden.

Perhaps a tear slips from your eye as you go to sleep, or a bit of frustration releases as you pace the hospital halls. While these small leaks reduce the pressure rising inside you, what you'd really like is a chance to let it all out.

Dear friend, you may feel trapped in this struggle, but remember that you can always rest in God's presence. The psalmist described his situation in dire terms—nearly drowning, unable to catch a foothold, worn out, and parched. And yet he ultimately found hope in his Savior.

That same God is here with you now, listening and waiting. He sees every burden you bear and longs to provide you comfort.

Will you let Him?

—⟋∿⟍—

Dear Lord,

This situation is far from easy, and I feel the pressure building inside. There's so much to process—so much going through my mind—but I can't show it with my care recipient nearby. It's unbearable to watch him struggle, and emotion sits beneath the surface, ready to burst out at any moment. I've tried to keep my feelings hidden, but the truth is, I'm not a robot. I'm a human being desperate for relief.

Lord, I'm so grateful that even if I never find an outlet here on earth, You offer a safe place to bring my cares. You meet me in these floodwaters and reach out to hold me. I turn to You now and lay it all at Your feet—every fear, hurt, and burden. They're not mine to carry, so I ask You to take them.

If I need more solitude to process what's happening, would You open windows in my schedule to do that? Even if it's just a few minutes of quiet, I want to come to You with my cares first. Help me recognize creative ways I can release my emotions, whether it's journaling, spending time in a coloring Bible, or going on prayer walks. If I need to reach out to a friend or counselor, give me humility to recognize that, and may our conversation be productive and healing.

I know I can't go through this hardship on my own, so I look to You for my comfort and help. You are a faithful God—a safe shelter in an unstable world. Thank You for meeting me here and listening. I choose to rest in You.

In Jesus's name, amen.

38

When You're Too Busy to Take Care of Yourself

For those who have neglected their own health while caring for someone else.

You can be sure that God will take care of everything you need, his generosity exceeding even yours in the glory that pours from Jesus.
PHILIPPIANS 4:19 MSG

—⁓—

You don't want to let your health slip, but it feels impossible. How can you take care of yourself when priorities pull you in so many directions?

You might be away from home, struggling to find any sort of routine, let alone a healthy one. Perhaps you're under immense stress, and the kitchen is your safe haven. You might have medical conditions of your own, but your care recipient's needs limit you from keeping doctor appointments or maintaining a healthy lifestyle.

Whatever the cause, rest assured that you're not alone. You may struggle to take care of yourself, but you have a heavenly Father who provides everything you need. When you lack inspiration, He can send a burst of creativity. When you need more time, He'll open your eyes to see the minutes you have. When your will-power fades, He'll help you run the race with perseverance (Hebrews 12:1).

The task ahead may not be easy, but God doesn't leave you to walk in your own strength. He's right by your side, pointing the way to a life of health and wholeness.

Will you let Him lead you?

———ᴍ———

Dear Lord,

I know I've been called to provide care in this season, but I'm struggling to tend to my health in the process. Time isn't my own anymore. Routines have been shaken, and stress has mounted. It's the least I can do to keep up with my own doctor appointments, let alone be proactive to exercise or eat well. It's hard to see opportunities when all I see are challenges ahead.

Even though it seems impossible, I'm grateful You know my struggle and offer help. You're a generous God who can provide far more than anyone on this earth, so I pray for vision to see You working.

Where opportunities exist to take better care of myself, would You open my eyes to see them? Whether it's wholesome snacks I can grab or locations nearby where I can walk, show me what's available and give me the willpower to follow through. I want to bring my best to caregiving, and that means doing whatever I can to stay healthy.

Help me entrust my time to You, no matter how small. I believe You can take my efforts and multiply them. When my motivation flags, I pray You will fill me with energy. I want to stay grounded in Your Word, so I come to You first when I'm tempted to give up.

If I need accountability to keep me on track, show me who might be close by. I know I'm not the only one struggling to take care of myself in the midst of a busy life. Enable me to see those who can link arms with me, and build a foundation of support among us.

Even though this season has humbled me, I'm grateful You can work in my weakness. I trust You to make Your power known, and I commit each choice to You.

In Jesus's name, amen.

39

When You're Transitioning from Hospital to Home

For those whose care recipient has been
discharged from the hospital.

*Every good and perfect gift is from above, coming down
from the Father of the heavenly lights, who does not
change like shifting shadows.*

JAMES 1:17

Finally, you've received the green light. After hours
in the hospital with your care recipient, you're free
to go.

Part of you is relieved to return somewhere comfortable, but another part is overwhelmed. No longer is the
hospital staff responsible for your care recipient's needs.
The primary job falls to you. Some days you feel up to

the task, but others you don't. All you can hope is that you stay strong.

My friend, whatever has happened to this point and whatever lies ahead, remember you have access to a God who is unchanging. He's the Giver of every good gift, including this transition from the hospital. He'll calm your anxious heart and clear your mind.

When fear seeps in, let His goodness wash it away. When exhaustion weighs you down, let Him lift it from your shoulders. He knows what comes next and offers His steady hand to hold you firm.

Will you turn to Him now?

———— ᴍ ————

Dear Lord,

I have mixed emotions as I transition home with my care recipient. Part of me is relieved that her condition has improved. It's a gift from You, and I thank You for it. But I'm also worried about what lies ahead. Being responsible for her care is a big job, and I don't want to do anything to cause a setback.

Many changes lie ahead, Lord, but I'm thankful You remain the same. When life's circumstances shift like shadows, moving me from one place to the next, You are constant. I may worry about what's ahead, but You're here to guide me.

As I look to You, I ask for strength. Not only do I need physical energy to keep up with the demands, but I need mental and emotional strength as well. If my care recipient struggles through the transition, help me be a calming presence in her life. Her condition impacts more than her body, so give me wisdom and patience to support her through every challenge.

I also lift up other relationships throughout this transition. Friends or family members in the home may be greatly impacted by this move, and I want us to grow closer rather than further apart. If children are present, help me explain what has happened in a way that can be understood and processed. Give me awareness every day to see those around me, whether my care recipient or other loved ones, and help me filter each response through the lens of Your love.

This season may bring joy or it may bring pain, but I rest in the peace You provide. No matter where life leads, You're steady and faithful. Thank You for guiding me and drawing my heart to Yours.

In Jesus's name, amen.

40

When You're Under Financial Stress

For those who don't know how they'll pay the bills.

Look at the birds. They don't plant or harvest or store food in barns, for your heavenly Father feeds them. And aren't you far more valuable to him than they are? Seek the Kingdom of God above all else, and live righteously, and he will give you everything you need.

MATTHEW 6:26,33 NLT

Anxiety cinches tight as you look at your pile of bills. You know simple math, and it says there's no way out of this mess.

Financial pressure may come from many directions. Perhaps your care recipient is your spouse or child, and you're not sure you can shoulder the burden of his medical costs. Maybe his health declined quickly, forcing you to leave your job or reduce your hours to provide care. Maybe you've been getting by, but other needs have pressed in at home, calling for income that isn't available.

Dear friend, whatever the cause of this angst, I pray you'll find hope in God's care. Scripture says He watches over the birds and plants, giving them food when they need it. They don't have endless reserves stored away, but they live each day in trust, knowing the Father will provide.

You, too, can live in daily trust that your needs will be met. In fact, you are deemed "far more valuable" to God than any other creature. He calls you to seek Him first, to rest in His presence and follow His way.

Will you trust Him now?

———⁓⁓———

Dear Lord,

I can't help but worry when I look at the bills coming in. Some of them are so big, it's hard to imagine how they can ever be paid. I'm working to make progress, but it feels like scooping a mountain of dirt with a teaspoon. How can I trust You for my needs when I see no way out?

I may not envision a way through this, but I'm

thankful You do. You care for the birds of the air, providing their food each day, and You see me as far more valuable. What a comforting reminder that I don't have to carry this burden alone.

As I evaluate my finances, would You give me wisdom to know what to pay first? If there are any bills that can be negotiated, help me contact the right people to make it happen. I ask for open dialogue with finance offices as I explore all the options and for clarity as I move forward.

I also pray for vision to see ways I can bring in extra income. My schedule is full, but I don't want to miss opportunities to ease the budget. Whether it's selling possessions, learning a new skill, or utilizing an old skill in a new way, give me mental and physical energy to pursue all possibilities.

No matter what happens in the long term, I place my trust in You today. I may not see how these bills will be paid, but I want this trial to draw me closer to You. You provide everything I need, and I rest in Your care.

In Jesus's name, amen.

41

When You're Waiting for Answers

For those anticipating test results for
someone under their care.

Who of you by worrying can add a single hour to your life?

LUKE 12:25

Cast your cares on the LORD and he will sustain you;
he will never let the righteous be shaken.

PSALM 55:22

———∭———

Time ticks by as you wait for answers. You know your care recipient's results have the power to change your life, but you're trying not to get ahead of yourself. For all you know, everything could be fine—a simple answer or routine explanation. But you also know nothing is guaranteed. If the answer isn't so simple, life could take a difficult turn.

Dear friend, as you sit in this pocket of the unknown, allow your worries to lift to your Savior. He sees what's going on in your care recipient. He knows the answers and diagnosis. Whether the hours ahead are easy or difficult, He'll be by your side.

Your world may be shaken, but you can always find hope in God. He invites you to cast your cares on Him, to set aside your worries and let His presence sustain you.

Will you do that now?

———

Dear Lord,

I feel as if I'm standing at the edge of a cliff, waiting to find out if I'll be shoved forward or allowed to walk safely back down the mountain. So many questions linger. *What will the doctors find? How will it impact my care recipient? How will it impact me? Am I up to the tasks that lie ahead?* I don't know the answers, but I trust You do.

While I'm stuck in the wondering, I'm thankful You already see. You're working and moving even in my uncertainty. When worries cloud my mind, help me turn them over to You. I recognize I can't add hours to my life by imagining the worst, so I choose to rest in this moment and trust Your plan.

As the minutes tick by, please keep me aware of those around me. I know my care recipient is battling fears of her own, and I want to be a solid support. Show me how I can comfort her, and draw us both to You in prayer. Let this be a time of sweet communion—not only with each other but also in Your presence. While we wait, I pray You will guide the doctors analyzing the results. Clear their vision to see the root cause, and give them wisdom to make the right diagnosis.

Whatever answer they bring, I choose to lean on You. If it's good news, let me declare Your praises. If it's bad news, help me proclaim Your goodness in hard times. I release every concern and trust You to strengthen me wherever You may lead.

In Jesus's name, amen.

42

When You've Lost Patience with God

For those who want their care recipient
to be healed right now.

*How long, LORD, must I call for help, but you do not listen?
Or cry out to you, "Violence!" but you do not save?*

<small>HABAKKUK 1:2</small>

*I have heard all about you, LORD. I am filled with
awe by your amazing works. In this time of our deep
need, help us again as you did in years gone by. And
in your anger, remember your mercy.*

<small>HABAKKUK 3:2 NLT</small>

———

Not yet. These two words ring in your ears, filling you with helplessness as you watch your care recipient suffer.

Maybe she's waiting for a lifesaving procedure that could be weeks away. Perhaps she sits next to you in a medical office, slumped in her chair while names are rattled off. Or maybe you've watched her deal with the same illness time and time again, visiting multiple doctors in hope of an answer. But the only words you hear are, "Not yet."

Whatever the situation, you've come to despise those two little words. If only you could speed the process along and relieve this suffering. And yet you remain powerless.

When impatience builds, dear friend, remember that God has a plan. It may not be clear, but just as He's provided for you in the past, He will do so again. As you open your heart to Him, He can calm it with peace and trust.

Will you allow Him to do that now?

—⁓—

Dear Lord,

I can't help but admit I'm tired of waiting. From sitting in yet another doctor's office to anticipating a cure for my care recipient, my patience is spent. It's tearing me apart to watch this suffering, and my life outside these circumstances feels broken while I focus my energy here. I wish I could snap my fingers and make life return to normal, but I know it's not possible.

In my moments of impatience, would You remind me of all the times You've been faithful in the past? I don't want this situation to harden my heart with bitterness, so I ask You to fill me with trust. Help me focus on what I can control in this situation and release the rest to You. Even though I don't understand Your timing, I believe You know what's best.

Thank You for the ways You're working, even when I can't see the big picture. While I wait, please show me how to turn my frustrations into praise. If there's something You want to change in me, give me wisdom and humility to admit where I can be remolded. If You want to use me to bless others who cross my path, open my eyes to see their needs.

Whether immediate healing comes or not, I place all my longings in Your hands. You're in control, and I trust You to work all things according to Your perfect plan.

In Jesus's name, amen.

43

When You've Lost Patience with Your Care Recipient

For those who've been tested to their limit.

You, O Lord, are a God of compassion and mercy, slow to get angry and filled with unfailing love and faithfulness.

PSALM 86:15 NLT

May God, who gives this patience and encouragement, help you live in complete harmony with each other, as is fitting for followers of Christ Jesus.

ROMANS 15:5 NLT

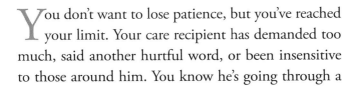

Y ou don't want to lose patience, but you've reached your limit. Your care recipient has demanded too much, said another hurtful word, or been insensitive to those around him. You know he's going through a lot, but it doesn't make it any easier to be on the receiving end.

When frustration mounts, you might stuff it inside, tossing it onto a pile of other past hurts. Perhaps it spills out in harsh words or actions. After the moment passes, you feel guilty, and yet there seems to be no other option. You're placed in a lose-lose situation, trying to help someone but feeling like his punching bag in the process.

My friend, when you reach the end of your patience, remember God can fill you with His. He is full of compassion and mercy. He doesn't rush to show anger but instead offers a boundless supply of love. When this situation tests every part of you, let your heavenly Father transform your mind and spirit. He longs to help you live in harmony.

Will you let Him?

———

Dear Lord,

So much is tested as I watch my care recipient suffer. Oftentimes he takes his frustration out on me, and it builds up inside me like a volcano, ready to erupt. I try to stay calm, and many times I succeed. But other times

I lose my cool and say things I regret. I know my care recipient is facing fear and discouragement right now. This trial is far from easy, and I recognize that. I want to do all I can to help, but I also long for kindness.

If I have allowed him to treat me in an unhealthy way, give me courage to stand up for myself. I don't want to arrogantly command respect, so I ask for Your grace to speak through me. Guide any conversations that need to take place, and allow us to reach a mutual understanding.

If my impatience has boiled over in hurtful ways, fill me with humility to recognize my errors. The last thing I want is to perpetuate this cycle, so I pray You would shape me and restore what's broken. When I face moments of testing, would You turn my eyes to You? I'm so grateful for Your compassion and mercy. You're the perfect model of patience, and I want a full portion of what You offer.

Whatever comes, I accept this opportunity to rely on You. I long to be a person of patience, encouragement, and love, and I trust You to fill me.

In Jesus's name, amen.

44

When You've Lost Your Identity

For those whose identity is stripped away
by someone else's struggle.

*O LORD, you have examined my heart and know everything
about me. You know when I sit down or stand up. You
know my thoughts even when I'm far away. You see me
when I travel and when I rest at home. You know everything
I do. You know what I am going to say even before I say it,
LORD. You go before me and follow me. You place your hand
of blessing on my head.*

PSALM 139:1-5 NLT

L ines blur as you pour into your care recipient day
after day. His struggle becomes yours, and you're not
sure who you are anymore. With each passing moment,
your former life feels like a distant memory—activities
you enjoyed, people who shaped you, work that defined

you. Now you track time by doctor appointments and hours between medications.

My friend, as you face this unsettling place, allow yourself to rest in the arms of your all-knowing God. Others may fail to recognize the core of who you are, but He always sees. He created you with care and precision. He orchestrated each season of your life, even this difficult one.

When you feel lost in the struggle, remember you're not alone. God not only knows who you are deep inside, but He's placed His hand of blessing on you. He will restore pieces of your identity in His perfect timing.

Will you trust Him to do that?

———

Dear Lord,

I've lost so many parts of myself as I travel deeper into caregiving. Things I used to love don't fit in my schedule anymore. People I spent time with are either gone or unable to be with me now. Activities and work I poured myself into have all faded in the shadow of this struggle. And with them, my identity has faded too. I know I'm where You want me to be, but I still long for glimpses of my former life—just a small taste of the joys and friendships.

Whether my old identity is restored or not, Lord, I'm grateful You haven't lost sight of who I am. You designed every part of me—the pieces that seem distant and the pieces that fill my life now. They may look fragmented to me, but I trust You're crafting them into a masterful mosaic.

As I face each day, would You open my eyes to see the color around me? My life may have changed, but that doesn't mean You're not working. Keep me aware of Your goodness, and let me use this time to praise You. If there are opportunities to bring former activities or people into my life, help me see what's nearby. I don't want to get so bogged down in my struggle that I neglect the unique ways You've made me.

Whether my life returns to normal or not, I'm grateful for what You're doing here and now. This role has changed me forever, and I want it to be for Your glory. As I seek to bridge the gap between past and present, let my actions point others to You.

Thank You for being the Lord of every season. What an honor to be known by You and to have Your hand of blessing. No matter what comes, I place my identity in You alone.

In Jesus's name, amen.

45

When You've Reached the End of Your Care Recipient's Life

For those who will soon lose someone close to them.

I am convinced that nothing can ever separate us from God's love. Neither death nor life, neither angels nor demons, neither our fears for today nor our worries about tomorrow—not even the powers of hell can separate us from God's love. No power in the sky above or in the earth below—indeed, nothing in all creation will ever be able to separate us from the love of God that is revealed in Christ Jesus our Lord.

ROMANS 8:38-39 NLT

———

Nothing reminds you of the frailty of life more than the nearness of death. It's not easy to acknowledge, but you've known this time would come.

Conflicting emotions may war within you as you

face the days ahead. If your care recipient's condition worsened quickly, you may struggle with disbelief and a numb grief that hasn't sunk in yet. If she's been ill for a long time, you've expected this moment, but it still doesn't make it easy. Maybe the process has been so long and difficult that you've secretly longed for relief, only to discover that guilt now haunts you. Perhaps you face a slew of logistical details to iron out, and you're overwhelmed by it all.

None of these struggles touches the deepest part of you—the part that considers what happens after death. You might be unsure if your care recipient has made a decision of faith in Christ, and you worry it's too late. Or maybe she's confident in her eternal home, but you're not sure you'll be there with her someday. Perhaps you know you'll both be in heaven together again, but you dread the heartache in the meantime.

Dear friend, as all these emotions swell within you, I pray you'll find release in the arms of God. The Bible says nothing can keep you from His love. He reaches past death, darkness, fear, and worry to meet you where you are. When the world shakes with uncertainty, He's a steadying force. When you question the future, He promises an eternal hope.

Will you look to Him now?

—〰—

Dear Lord,

It's hard to describe the depth of emotion I'm facing right now. Sometimes it feels like a clamp is squeezing my chest, unrelenting as I go about my day. My mind rarely strays from the loss that's looming, and I waver between many thoughts and struggles.

I'm thankful that in this hard situation, You reach out to me with a deep, deep love. You see every moment—the times I feel numb, scared, weary, and overwhelmed—and You draw me close.

I ask for greater awareness of Your presence during the days to come. As I wrap up loose ends, give me a clear head in the midst of my grief. When sadness or fear seeps in, help me rest in You. I trust You to lift me with Your strength when exhaustion weighs me down.

The journey to this point hasn't been easy, and I find myself reflecting on the past. If there are words or actions that have created a rift in my relationship with my care recipient, help me use these final days to acknowledge my part and make it right. Even if I'm unable to reconcile with her now, I ask for peace as I seek Your forgiveness.

Lord, thank You for the promise of heaven beyond

this life. If there are any decisions left unmade—either by my care recipient or myself—I come to You with an open heart and ask that all barriers be removed. I acknowledge Jesus as my Savior, and I choose to follow You from this moment forward.

The coming days may bring uncertainty and pain, but I'm grateful You're with me, guiding me through. I cling to You now and trust in Your promise of hope and a future.

In Jesus's name, amen.

46

When You've Reached the End of Your Caregiving

For those transitioning back to normal life.

There is a season (a time appointed) for everything and a time for every delight and event or purpose under heaven—a time to be born and a time to die; a time to plant and a time to uproot what is planted...a time to weep and a time to laugh; a time to mourn and a time to dance.
ECCLESIASTES 3:1-2,4 AMP

Jesus Christ is the same yesterday and today and forever.
HEBREWS 13:8

————

After weeks, months, or years of caregiving, you're free to return to normal life. And yet, you can't remember what normal is anymore.

Emotions play teeter-totter in your heart as you

think about the future. Grief is present when you miss precious moments with your care recipient. Joy seeps in when you're able to connect with friends and family who didn't fit in your schedule before. Lack of purpose may leave you listless as you wonder what to do with yourself next. The phrase "a season for everything" certainly resonates, and you're not sure which way to turn.

Dear friend, wherever you find yourself today, I pray you sense the presence of your unchanging God. He offers comfort when you're overwhelmed with sadness. He renews relationships that have taken a back seat during your caregiving. And He longs to give you renewed purpose and hope.

Whatever this next season brings, your heavenly Father remains the same. He's ready and waiting to give what you need.

Will you let Him?

―――∭―――

Dear Lord,

I've taken a turn on the road of life, and nothing looks familiar anymore. Sometimes I find myself enjoying the beauty here. Other times I feel lost. Part of me misses the previous routine, but I want to embrace this new phase and all You have for me.

Thank You for the reminder that You're the same yesterday, today, and forever. You oversee all the stages of life and know what I need in each one. As I move forward, would You remind me of Your presence? It's tempting to forge ahead on my own, but I need You in this season just as much as the last.

If logistics need to be handled as I transition out of caregiving, please give me focus and energy to complete them. Grief often lingers under the surface, so I look to You for my comfort each day.

When loneliness sets in, help me reach out for support. You offer everything I need, but You've also provided people to walk through life by my side. If friendships or family have been put on hold, I ask for opportunities to reconnect. I want to embrace this time and allow You to fill me with joy.

I also pray for clarity and purpose as I move forward. My schedule is much different than it used to be, and sometimes I don't know what to do with myself. As I draw close to You, I trust You will guide me and reveal opportunities. Show me new doors of ministry, and give me fresh excitement to follow Your will.

If there are ways I can take better care of myself, please make that clear and give me strength to make the necessary changes. If I need to rest in solitude for a while, release my desire for control and allow me to refill my energy in Your presence.

Whatever comes, I look forward to exploring this path before me. It may be new and unfamiliar, but You're right by my side, leading the way. I choose to follow You in each step.

In Jesus's name, amen.

About the Author

Sarah Forgrave is an author and speaker who loves encouraging others toward a deeper walk of faith. As someone who has spent considerable time in doctors' offices, both as a patient and caregiver, Sarah knows the challenges and triumphs a health journey can bring. Her greatest passion is connecting with God in the messes and hardships of life.

She is the author of *Prayers for Hope and Healing*, a prayer devotional for those facing health challenges. Her work has also been featured in *The Gift of Friendship*, Guideposts' *A Cup of Christmas Cheer*, and *Mother of Pearl: Luminous Lessons and Iridescent Faith*. Outside of writing and speaking, Sarah is the busy mom of two children and the wife of an entrepreneurial husband. When she has a moment to herself, she loves to shop the aisles at Trader Joe's or curl up with a good book and a cup of tea.

Sarah blogs at www.sarahforgrave.com. She can also be found on…

Pinterest: www.pinterest.com/SarahForgrave

Facebook: www.facebook.com/AuthorSarahForgrave

Instagram: SarahForgrave_author

Twitter: @SarahForgrave

Acknowledgments

This book was a team effort from beginning to end. Special thanks go to:

My Redeemer and Lord—You're the ultimate source of hope and comfort. Thank You for filling me with strength when I feel weak.

The publishing team at Harvest House—What an honor to partner with you in ministry. Thank you for caring for all the details with such skill, from cover to binding and everything in between. Special thanks to Todd Hafer for championing my work and to Kim Moore for polishing my manuscripts with grace and a smile.

My agent, Cynthia Ruchti—I'm so grateful you've taken me under your wing. Your wisdom and encouragement have been invaluable. And to my former agent, Mary Keeley—thank you for steering the way to make this book possible. What a gift to have both of you in my life.

My husband, Jeff—Where would I be without your support? So many times you've taken on a caregiving role for me and have done so without complaint. I'm grateful, and I love you.

My parents and stepparents—Thank you, Mom and Dad, for working tirelessly, especially during our family's cancer years, and for making the road feel less bumpy than it actually was. And to my stepparents for joining our family and cheering me on.

My sister, Jenny—Thank you for allowing me to be an integral part in your heart transplant journey. We've come through so much, and now we get to help others yet again. What an honor!

My in-laws—You've been fantastic on-call babysitters and all-around cheerleaders throughout my journey. A thousand thank-yous!

My hometown prayer team (Jen C., Sue F., Sarah C., Judy C., and Patti R.)—Each one of you is such a BLESSING. Patti, thank you for giving me an additional chapter to include. Judy and Sue, thank you for sharing your hearts and caregiving struggles at our breakfast at Panera. You renewed my fervor for writing this book.

My friend Amelia Rhodes—I'm so grateful for your prayer and ministry partnership. It's always a joy to see your Monday texts.

The CP Care Team and Library Ministry—Thank you for standing behind me and spreading hope in our community.

All my friends who have supported, championed, encouraged, liked, tweeted, reviewed, endorsed, and everything in between throughout my publishing journey—You keep me going!

Amid Pain and Weakness...There Is HOPE

Serious or chronic medical issues bring a litany of painful and confusing feelings that only someone else who's been in a similar situation could possibly understand. Sarah Forgrave has walked the difficult road you find yourself on. And she empathizes with the uncertain future you face.

No matter the road ahead, you don't have to face it alone. Even in the depths of your worst emotional and physical pain, God is right there beside you, offering His comfort, love, and peace.

As you read these heartfelt prayers and devotions, let this book be your manual to help navigate the difficult set of emotions that come with health issues. Read it front to back or go directly to the devotion addressing how you feel at any given moment...when you need it the most.

Above all, know that you are never, ever alone.

To learn more about Harvest House books and
to read sample chapters, visit our website:

www.harvesthousepublishers.com

HARVEST HOUSE PUBLISHERS
EUGENE, OREGON